TABLE OF CONTENTS

Unless otherwise indicated, all Scripture quotations are taken from the King James Version of the Bible.
The Making of a Champion
ISBN 1-56394-163-5/B-59
Copyright © 2002 by **MIKE MURDOCK**
All publishing rights belong exclusively to Wisdom International
Publisher/Editor: Deborah Murdock Johnson
Published by The Wisdom Center · 4051 Denton Hwy. · Ft. Worth, Texas 76117
1-817-759-BOOK · 1-817-759-0300
You Will Love Our Website...! WisdomOnline.com

Accuracy Department: To our Friends and Partners...We welcome any comments on errors or misprints you find in our book...Email our department: AccuracyDept@thewisdomcenter.tv. Your aid in helping us excel is highly valued.

Champions Make Decisions
That Create The Future
They Desire; Losers Make
Decisions That Create
The Present They Desire.

-MIKE MURDOCK

WHY I WROTE THIS BOOK

━━━━━━━━⟫▪◉▪⟪━━━━━━━━

A Champion—*Webster's New Collegiate Dictionary defines* a Champion as "one who shows marked superiority." There are not many words that could describe being a Champion better than that. It has been said that Champions aren't born, they are *made—one day at a time.* And that is what this book is all about—making yourself into a Champion.

After years of pursuing God's best for my life, I have discovered God's principles for being a Champion. The quotes, Wisdom Keys and principles found on these pages will inspire and equip you to fulfill your Assignment. You will learn to always reach for the best in life and not settle for less; to stand out from the crowd and not accept mediocrity. *You will become a Champion.*

That's why I wrote this book.

Mike Murdock

The Word of God Is
The Wisdom
of God.

-MIKE MURDOCK

≈ 1 ≈

RECOGNIZE THAT THE WORD OF GOD IS THE WISDOM OF GOD

The Bible Is The Master Success Handbook.

Your most difficult life-habit to birth will be reading The Word of God every morning of your life. Yet, it is the Miracle Tool that produces changes your heart longs for.

12 Rewards of Reading The Word of God

1. The Word of God Unleashes Your Very Life Within You. "It is the Spirit that quickeneth; the flesh profiteth nothing: the words that I speak unto you, they are spirit, and they are life," (John 6:63). Life is energy. The Word of God creates unexplainable energy. "...quicken me according to Thy judgments," (Psalm 119:156).

2. The Word of God Solves Your Mental Problems. "Great peace have they which love Thy law," (Psalm 119:165).

3. The Word of God Cleanses Your Conscience. "Now ye are clean through the Word which I have spoken unto you," (John 15:3).

4. The Word of God Purifies. "Wherewithal shall a young man cleanse his way? by taking heed thereto according to Thy word," (Psalm 119:9).

5.   The Word of God Corrects You.   "All scripture is given by inspiration of God, and is profitable for doctrine, for reproof, for correction, for instruction in righteousness," (2 Timothy 3:16).

6.   The Word of God Solves Every Battle. "Thou through Thy commandments hast made me wiser than mine enemies," (Psalm 119:98).

7.   The Word of God Warns of Pitfalls. "Thy word have I hid in mine heart, that I might not sin against Thee," (Psalm 119:11). "The wicked have laid a snare for me: yet I erred not from Thy precepts," (Psalm 119:110).

8.   The Word of God Drives Back The Darkness Around You. "The entrance of Thy words giveth light," (Psalm 119:130).

9.   The Word of God Births Uncommon Joy. "These things have I spoken unto you, that My joy might remain in you, and that your joy might be full," (John 15:11).

10.   The Word of God Births The Fear of God. Examples of judgment energizes us to correct our conduct and change our behavior.

11.   The Word of God Creates A Hatred of Evil. "Be not wise in thine own eyes: fear the Lord, and depart from evil," (Proverbs 3:7).

12.   The Word of God Is The Source of Wisdom In Your Life. "For the Lord giveth Wisdom; out of His mouth cometh knowledge and understanding," (Proverbs 2:6).

12 Rewards of Wisdom

1.   Wisdom Is The Master Key To All The Treasures of Life. "And God said to Solomon, Because this was in thine heart, and thou hast not asked riches, wealth, or honour, such as none of the kings have had that have been before," (2 Chronicles 1:11-12).

"In Whom are hid all the treasures of Wisdom and knowledge," (Colossians 2:3).

2. The Fear of God Is The Beginning of Wisdom. "The fear of the Lord is the beginning of Wisdom: and the knowledge of the holy is understanding," (Proverbs 9:10).

"The fear of the Lord is the beginning of Wisdom," (Psalm 111:10).

"And unto man He said, Behold, the fear of the Lord, that is Wisdom; and to depart from evil is understanding," (Job 28:28).

3. Wisdom Is More Powerful Than Weapons of War. "Wisdom is better than weapons of war," (Ecclesiastes 9:18). "And Wisdom and knowledge shall be the stability of thy times, and strength of salvation: the fear of the Lord is His treasure," (Isaiah 33:6).

"But the mouth of the upright shall deliver them," (Proverbs 12:6).

4. Right Relationships Increase Your Wisdom. "He that walketh with wise men shall be wise: but a companion of fools shall be destroyed," (Proverbs 13:20).

"Be not deceived: evil communications corrupt good manners," (1 Corinthians 15:33).

"Perverse disputings of men of corrupt minds, and destitute of the truth, supposing that gain is godliness: from such withdraw thyself," (1 Timothy 6:5).

5. Wisdom Is Better Than Jewels Or Money. "For Wisdom is better than rubies; and all the things that may be desired are not to be compared to it," (Proverbs 8:11).

"Happy is the man that findeth Wisdom, and the

man that getteth understanding. For the merchandise of it is better than the merchandise of silver, and the gain thereof than fine gold. She is more precious than rubies; and all the things thou canst desire are not to be compared unto her," (Proverbs 3:13-15).

"...for the price of Wisdom is above rubies," (Job 28:18).

"How much better is it to get Wisdom than gold! and to get understanding rather than to be chosen than silver!" (Proverbs 16:16).

6.   The Wise Welcome Correction. "Reprove not a scorner, lest he hate thee: rebuke a wise man, and he will love thee. Give instruction to a wise man, and he will be yet wiser: teach a just man, and he will increase in learning," (Proverbs 9:8-9).

"The ear that heareth the reproof of life abideth among the wise. He that refuseth instruction despiseth his own soul: but he that heareth reproof getteth understanding," (Proverbs 15:31-32).

"My son, despise not the chastening of the Lord; neither be weary of His correction: For whom the Lord loveth He correcteth; even as a father the son in whom he delighteth," (Proverbs 3:11-12).

7.   Wisdom Creates Currents of Favor And Recognition Toward You. "Exalt her, and she shall promote thee: she shall bring thee to honour, when thou dost embrace her," (Proverbs 4:8).

"Blessed is the man that heareth Me, watching daily at My gates, waiting at the posts of My doors. For whoso findeth Me findeth life, and shall obtain favour of the Lord," (Proverbs 8:34-35).

"My son, forget not My law; So shalt thou find favour and good understanding in the sight of God and man," (Proverbs 3:1, 4).

8.   Wisdom Guarantees Promotion. "By Me

kings reign, and princes decree justice. By Me princes rule, and nobles, even all the judges of the earth," (Proverbs 8:15-16).

"And thou, Ezra, after the Wisdom of thy God, that is in thine hand, set magistrates and judges, which may judge all the people that are beyond the river, all such as know the laws of thy God; and teach ye them that know them not," (Ezra 7:25).

"Exalt her, and she shall promote thee: she shall bring thee to honour, when thou dost embrace her. She shall give to thine head an ornament of grace: a crown of glory shall she deliver to thee," (Proverbs 4:8-9).

9.   When You Increase Your Wisdom You Will Increase Your Wealth. "Riches and honour are with Me; yea, durable riches and righteousness. That I may cause those that love Me to inherit substance; and I will fill their treasures," (Proverbs 8:18, 21).

"Length of days is in her right hand; and in her left hand riches and honour," (Proverbs 3:16).

"Blessed is the man that feareth the Lord, that delighteth greatly in His commandments. Wealth and riches shall be in his house," (Psalm 112:1, 3).

"The crown of the wise is their riches," (Proverbs 14:24).

10. Wisdom Makes Your Enemies Helpless Against You. "For I will give you a mouth and Wisdom, which all your adversaries shall not be able to gainsay nor resist," (Luke 21:15).

"When a man's ways please the Lord, He maketh even his enemies to be at peace with him," (Proverbs 16:7).

"For Wisdom is a defence, and money is a defence," (Ecclesiastes 7:12).

"For the Lord giveth Wisdom:...to deliver thee from the way of evil man,...To deliver thee from the strange woman," (Proverbs 2:6, 12, 16).

11. Wisdom Can Be Imparted By The Laying On of Hands of A Man of God. "Wherefore I put thee in remembrance that thou stir up the gift of God, which is in thee by the putting on of my hands. That good thing which was committed unto thee keep by the Holy Ghost which dwelleth in us," (2 Timothy 1:6, 14).

"And Joshua the son of Nun was full of the Spirit of Wisdom; for Moses had laid his hands upon him," (Deuteronomy 34:9).

"Whom they set before the apostles: and when they had prayed, they laid their hands on them. And Stephen, full of faith and power, did great wonders and miracles among the people. And they were not able to resist the Wisdom and the Spirit by which he spake," (Acts 6:6, 8, 10).

12. The Word of God Is Your Source of Wisdom. "Behold, I have taught you statutes and judgments, even as the Lord my God commanded me, that ye should do so in the land whither ye go to possess it. For this is your Wisdom and your understanding in the sight of the nations," (Deuteronomy 4:5-6).

"Thou through Thy commandments hast made me wiser than mine enemies: for they are ever with me. I have more understanding than all my teachers: for Thy testimonies are my meditation. I understand more than the ancients, because I keep Thy precepts," (Psalm 119:98-100).

"For the Lord giveth Wisdom: out of His mouth cometh knowledge and understanding," (Proverbs 2:6).

9 Helpful Hints In Reading The Word of God

1. **Read It Daily.** What You Do *Daily* Determines What You Become Permanently.

2. **Read It Prayerfully.** The Holy Spirit will talk to you through His Word as you read it with a humble heart.

3. **Read It Thoughtfully.** Do not rush through it. Read each word as if it is pregnant with a secret coded message just for you. It is!

4. **Read It Joyfully.** Something is changing within you as His Word enters you. The words of God are like time-release capsules entering the soil of your life, releasing incredible benefits and pleasure.

5. **Read It Aloud.** When I read The Word of God aloud, it affects me more than at any other time. Sometimes, as a cassette tape of Scripture reading is playing, I will follow the reading along visually in my Bible. The effect is astounding. It multiplies the impact of the Word in your life.

6. **Mark The Bible As You Read It.** Color-code the Scriptures that mean the most to you. I use *red* to highlight Scriptures relating to the heartbeat of my life—The Holy Spirit, Jesus and The Word of God. Highlighted in *green* are the Scriptures related to financial blessing. *Yellow* indicates Scriptures I have already memorized or desire to memorize. *Blue* indicates something of uncommon importance.

7. **Wrap Every Telephone Conversation With A Scripture And Prayer.** Your emphasis on The Word of God may be the only time your friend hears it.

8. **Give The Word of God As Special Gifts To Those You Love.** That is why I created the

Topical Bibles for Businessmen, Fathers, Mothers and Teenagers. I created an entire series called the "One Minute Pocket Bible" for Mothers, Fathers and Businessmen. Nothing is more important than the Word.

9. Every Battle Against Your Life From Satan Is Designed To Separate You From The Word of God. When satan alienates you from the Word, he has destroyed your only effective Defense.

Your Most Important Friend Is The One Who Helps You Believe And Live The Word of God.

Your Worst Enemy Is Anyone Who Weakens Your Desire To Know And Obey The Word of God.

Recognition of The Word of God As Your Master Success Handbook Will Alter Your Behavior, Prepare You For Heaven And Unleash Uncommon Passion For Life.

Recognize That The Word of God Is The Wisdom of God.

This is one of the Secrets of Champions.

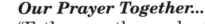 ***Our Prayer Together...***
"Father, use the words of this book as Seeds of greatness planted in the soil of Your people.

Remind us of Your greatness, our need of You and the access You have provided.

"Holy Spirit, You are the Source of uncommon joy, uncommon peace and uncommon Wisdom.

"Burn these words into our lives like the branding iron on a newborn calf.

"Expose every falsehood.

"Remove every enemy.

"Change us through Your Word.

"In Jesus' Name. Amen."

≈ 2 ≈

SET GOALS AND UPDATE THEM CONTINUOUSLY

━━━━▶-◦-◀━━━━

Decide What You Really Want.

In 1952 a prominent university discovered that only 3 out of 100 graduates had written down a clear list of goals. Ten years later, their follow-up study showed that 3 percent of the graduating class had accomplished more financially than the remaining 97 percent of the class.

Those 3 percent were the *same graduates* who had *written down their goals.* "Write the vision, and make it plain upon the tables, that he may run that readeth it," (Habakkuk 2:2).

When you decide exactly *"what"* you want, the *"how to do it"* will emerge.

Jesus knew His purpose and mission. "For the Son of man is come to seek and to save that which was lost," (Luke 19:10).

He knew the product He had to offer. "The thief cometh not, but for to steal, and to kill, and to destroy: I am come that they might have life, and that they might have it more abundantly," (John 10:10).

Jesus had a sense of destiny. He knew where He wanted to go. He knew where people needed Him. (See John 4:3.)

Jesus knew that achievers were detail-oriented. "For which of you, intending to build a tower, sitteth not down first, and counteth the cost, whether he have sufficient to finish it?" (Luke 14:28).

Take 4 sheets of paper. At the top of sheet number one, write, "My Lifetime Dreams And Goals."

Now write in total detail everything you would like to become, do, or have during your lifetime. *Dream your dreams in detail on paper.*

Now, take sheet number two and write, "My 12 Month Goals."

Now list everything you want to get done within the next 12 months.

Now, take the third sheet of paper and write, "My 30 Day Goals."

Now write out in detail what you would like to accomplish for the next 30 days.

Now take a fourth sheet of paper and write, "My Ideal Success Daily Routine."

Now write down the 6 most important things you will do in the next 24 hours.

The Secret of Your Future Is Hidden In Your Daily Routine. Set your goals.

Your goals will change throughout your life.

Someday, you will look back at this very moment and be amazed at the goals you presently have. Things so vital to you at 20 years of age will become unimportant to you at 30.

When I was beginning my ministry, I wanted very much to minister in many different states and cities. Times have changed. Today, staying home excites me. Knowing that my books are being read in many places is far more satisfying to me than traveling. The greatest goal of my life today is staying in my Secret Place of prayer and writing what The Holy Spirit teaches me through His Word and daily experiences.

These kinds of good changes will happen to you, too.

Here Are 6 Helpful Tips Concerning Your Dreams And Goals

1.   Invest One Hour In Writing Down Clearly The Goals That Really Matter To You At This Point. Keep it confidential and private, "Write the vision, and make it plain upon the tables, that he may run that readeth it," (Habakkuk 2:2).

2.   Permit Unexciting Dreams of Yesterday To Die. Stop pursuing something that does not have the ability to excite you anymore.   Do not feel obligated to keep trying to obtain it...if you are in a different place in your life. (See Isaiah 43:18-19.)

3.   Do Not Depend On Others To Understand Your Dreams And Goals. Permit them their individuality, also. They have every right to love the things they love.   But refuse to be intimidated by their efforts to persuade you to move in a different direction with your life.

4.   Never Make Permanent Decisions Because of Temporary Feelings. One young lady got so excited about a new friend, she dropped the lease on her own apartment and moved into the apartment of her friend. Within a week, she realized her mistake!

5.   Avoid Intimate Relationships With Those Who Do Not Really Respect Your Dreams. You will have to sever ties. *Wrong people do not* *always leave your life voluntarily.* Life is too short to permit discouragers close to you. "And have no fellowship with the unfruitful works of darkness, but rather reprove them," (Ephesians 5:11).

6. Anticipate Changes In Your Goals. Your present feelings and opinions are not permanent. New experiences are coming. New relationships are ahead. Stay conscious of this.

When you assess and evaluate your goals, you will unclutter your life of the unnecessary.

Set Goals And Update Them Continuously.

This is one of the Secrets of Champions.

RECOMMENDED INVESTMENTS:
Dream Seeds (Book/B-11/106 pages/$12)
Seeds of Wisdom on Dreams & Goals (Book/B-13/32 pages/$5)
Secrets of The Journey, Volume 7 (Book/B-103/32 pages/$5)

❧ 3 ❧

ANTICIPATE AND AVOID UNNECESSARY CONFLICT

Most Battles Are Not Really Important.

Here Are 16 Important Facts About Conflicts And Contentious People

1. Conflict Distracts You From Your Dreams And Goals. By the way, a contentious person often considers himself very honest and up front. In fact, they usually take pride in telling you "the way things really are." Subconsciously, they are often modeling someone in their life (a father or mother) who accomplished their goals through *intimidation.* Subconsciously, they admire this person and have decided to follow that pattern, failing to see the *losses* created through this kind of attitude.

2. Nothing Is More Harmful To A Company Than A Contentious Employee. Every boss knows this. When an employee cannot get along with other employees, profits are lost. That employee becomes costly. Focus is broken. Other employees become emotionally fragmented. Important projects are delayed.

3. Contentious People Destroy The Momentum, Bonding And Synergy That Agreement Can Create. "Mark them which cause divisions and offenses…avoid them," (Romans 16:17).

"And the servant of the Lord must not strive; but be gentle unto all men, apt to teach, patient," (2 Timothy 2:24).

4. Contentious People Are In Total Opposition To The Law of Agreement, The Greatest Law of Success On Earth. "Two are better than one; because they have a good reward for their labour. For if they fall, the one will lift up his fellow: but woe to him that is alone when he falleth; for he hath not another to help him up," (Ecclesiastes 4:9-10).

5. The Character of A Contentious Person Is Only Revealed When You Rebuke Them. If he is a scorner and fool, he will hate you. If he is a wise person simply needing correction, he will love you. "Reprove not a scorner, lest he hate thee: rebuke a wise man, and he will love thee," (Proverbs 9:8).

6. Contentious People Discuss Situations That Do Not Involve Them. This is one of the evidences of a contentious person. They discuss the business of *others*. "He that passeth by, and meddleth with strife belonging not to him, is like one that taketh a dog by the ears," (Proverbs 26:17).

7. A Contentious Person Enjoys Debate, Disputings And Opposing Whatever Has Been Spoken. A contentious person always looks for a reason to disagree about something. They *ignore* every point of *agreement*.

8. A Contentious Person Is Always A Door For Satan To Launch Every Evil Work In An Organization. "For where envying and strife is, there is confusion and every evil work," (James 3:16).

9. A Contentious Person Is In Opposition To Godly Wisdom. "But the Wisdom that is from above is first pure, then peaceable, gentle, and easy to be intreated, full of mercy and good fruits, without partiality, and without hypocrisy," (James 3:17).

10. A Contentious Attitude And Spirit Is Always Birthed By Unthankfulness. It is a sin that God abhors. It was the first sin ever committed. Satan was unthankful for his position and chose to fight for a change. *Ingratitude is poisonous.* It can destroy a family within weeks. It can ruin a successful organization within months. Churches exploding with growth have fragmented within weeks when a spirit of ingratitude infected the congregation.

11. Any Contentious Conversation Must Be Boldly Faced And Stopped Immediately. Interrupt the conversation with, "It is wonderful how God will *turn this* for our good! I am so thankful for what He is about to do! Do not we have a wonderful God!" It will be like throwing cold water on a destructive fire.

12. The Contentious Person Must Be Confronted Honestly And Courageously About Their Attitude. Others are bold enough to poison your climate and atmosphere with Arrows of Unthankfulness piercing the air. So, dominate your turf. Take charge. Use *your* words to turn the tide.

13. Contentious People Often Sabotage The Work of God. Many years ago I heard one of the most startling statements from a famous missionary. I was sitting under some huge trees in East Africa. Monkeys were jumping from tree limb to tree limb. My precious missionary friend explained the number one reason some missionaries never fulfill their full term on the field. (I thought missionaries came home due to sickness, culture shock or lack of finances.) "Mike, the number one reason missionaries do not stay on the mission field is their *inability to get along with other missionaries."* Think about it. Missionaries who should be obsessed with sharing the Gospel, often return home because of the failure to create harmony and an environment of agreement.

14. Contention Is Contagious. When someone permits the spirit of conflict and disputing to enter their life, they will influence and affect *everyone around them.* I have seen a happy, peaceful household dissolve into arguments within 30 minutes of the arrival of a contentious person. That person *carried* the spirit of contention with them.

15. Any Contentious Person Who Refuses To Change Must Not Continue To Have Access To You. "Where no wood is, there the fire goeth out: so where there is no talebearer, the strife ceaseth. As coals are to burning coals, and wood to fire; so is a contentious man to kindle strife," (Proverbs 26:20-21). *Your attitude is a personal decision.* Your attitude is a mood created by your chosen focus.

16. You Can Succeed Almost Anywhere Else, Except With A Contentious Person. "It is better to dwell in the corner of the housetop, than with a brawling woman and in a wide house," (Proverbs 25:24).

Remember, conflict always begins with a person, not merely an issue. "Where no wood is, there the fire goeth out: so where there is no talebearer, the strife ceaseth," (Proverbs 26:20). Agreement is the greatest enemy satan has ever faced. Walk away from contentious people.

Anticipate And Avoid Unnecessary Conflict.
This is one of the Secrets of Champions.

～ 4 ～

HABITUALIZE ORDER

Success Comes Through Small Steps.
Order and organizing your life is one of these important steps.

Here Are 8 Important Facts About Order And Organizing Your Life

1. Order Is The Accurate Arrangement of Things. Order is placing an item where it belongs. Order is keeping your shirts, ties and shoes in the appropriate place in your closet.

2. You Were Created For Order. Anything that slows you down emotionally or mentally will become a distraction.

3. Order Increases Comfort. When you walk into a room of order, you want to stay. Things are "right." You feel clean, energized and happy. When you walk into a room of clutter and disorder, an unexplainable agitation begins. Perhaps you cannot even name it or understand it.

4. When You Increase Order In Your Life, You Will Increase Your Productivity. Filing cabinets, trays on the desk and special places for folders make it easier to get your job done on *time*.

5. Order Eliminates Stress And Agitation. Have you ever shuffled paper after paper in search of a bill? Of course! When you finally located the bill, you were agitated and angry. It affected your entire day.

Disorder influences your attitude more than you could ever imagine.

6. Every Tiny Act of Your Life Will Increase Order Or Disorder Around You.

7. Everything You Are Doing Is Affecting Order In Your Life. Think for a moment. You get up from your breakfast table. Either you will leave your plate on the table, or you will take it to the sink. The decision you make will either increase the order or disorder around you. (Leaving it on the table increases your work load and creates disorder. Taking it to the sink *immediately* brings *order.*)

It happened last night to me. I took off my suit coat and laid it over the chair. I didn't really feel like taking it over to the closet and hanging it up. However, realizing that I was going to have to hang it up sooner or later, I walked over to the closet and hung up my coat. *I increased order* around myself immediately.

▶ Every moment you are increasing order or creating disorder around your life.

▶ Small tiny actions can eventually produce chaotic situations.

8. Every Person Around You Is Increasing Order Or Disorder. Some have an *attitude* of disorder. They are unhappy unless everything is in disarray and cluttered. Others refuse to work in such an environment. Their productivity requires organization.

Somebody has said that the arrangement of

things in your garage reveals much about your mind. Somebody asked me once, "Does this mean if I do not have a garage, that I really do not have a mind either?" (Smile!) I certainly hope that is not the case, but I am certain psychologists have come to some pretty accurate conclusions.

Why do we permit disorder?

1. Many of Us Were Raised With Those Who Are Unorganized. Large families, busy lifestyles or small, cramped apartments can contribute to our attitude.

2. Some People Do Not Know How To Separate And Organize Various Items Around Them. They need assistance.

3. Some People Have Unusual Sensitivity And Are Simply Gifted In Keeping Order Around Them.

4. Creative People Are Often Disorganiz-ed People. Their focus is change, not permanence. Their attention is on their future, not their present.

5. Busy People Moving From Place To Place Are Often Disorganized. Their mind is on where they are *going* instead of *where they are.*

Some helpful hints:

Recognize the long-term chaos and losses that disorder will create. If this continues, your momentum will eventually destroy you and your productivity. Successes will become fewer.

Take a long, hard and serious look at your personality and what you can do to take steps toward change.

Ask others who are gifted in organization to assist you and keep you on course. (I read where Donald

Trump said that he hired one woman whose entire job is to keep things in order around him.)

Do not berate yourself and become overly critical because of your lack of knowledge, giftings or ability to keep things in order.

Recognize those who God puts close to you who can correct things around you and keep things in order.

Do not try to justify yourself. Relax.

Take a small, tiny step today toward putting things around you in order.

It is commendable that you are planning to take an entire week of your vacation to put everything in order in your house next summer. However, I suggest you begin *this very moment* taking some steps to put things in place there in the room.

Just 20 minutes makes a major difference. Little hinges swing big doors. *You Can Get Anywhere You Want To Go If You Are Willing To Take Enough Small Steps.*

So, take an important step toward order every moment of your life.

Habitualize Order.

This is one of the Golden Secrets of Champions.

RECOMMENDED INVESTMENT:
Seeds of Wisdom on Habits (Book/B-18/32 pages/$3)

∞ 5 ∞

USE WORDS THAT MATTER IN EVERY CONVERSATION

Make Your Words Count.

Here Are 7 Facts You Should Remember In Every Conversation

1. **Avoid Sloppy Casual Conversation.** Pronounce your words clearly. Enunciate every single phrase to the best of your ability. Each conversation you enter is a practice session for excellence. It is too late to work on excellence when you walk onto a public platform. "For by thy words thou shalt be justified, and by thy words thou shalt be condemned," (Matthew 12:37).

2. **Never Speak When Another Person Is Talking.** It takes away from the value of your own words. If someone interrupts you while you are speaking, do not insist on being heard. Rather, say nothing. Permit them to speak.

3. **Qualify Others Before Speaking The Secrets of Your Heart.** Withhold your opinion until someone who values it shows up. "A word fitly spoken is like apples of gold in pictures of silver," (Proverbs 25:11).

4. **Speak Loud Enough For Others To**

Hear Clearly What You Are Saying. Do not mumble.

    5. Never Assume Others Have Understood What You Have Said. Sometimes, people are thinking about many other things while you are talking. Their mind is *not* on your words. They can be nodding in total agreement with your words, while their thoughts are a thousand miles away.

    6. Encourage Others To Speak Clearly. When others mutter or mumble, speak aloud and say, "I did not understand. Please repeat your words."

    7. Always Invest The Necessary Time In Searching For The Right Word, Even In The Midst of A Conversation. *Right* words are worth the time involved in finding them. *Wrong* words are devastating enough to avoid.

    Making your words count *in every conversation* will increase your skills dramatically.

47 Facts About Words

    1. Words Can Poison And Destroy A Young Man's Entire Life. (Read Proverbs 7.)

    2. Right Advice Guarantees Safety And Protection. "In the multitude of counsellors, there is safety," (Proverbs 11:14).

    3. Any Man Who Controls His Mouth Is Literally Protecting His Own Life. "He that keepeth his mouth keepeth his life," (Proverbs 13:3).

    4. Those Who Talk Too Much Will Eventually Be Destroyed. "He that openeth wide his lips shall have destruction," (Proverbs 13:3).

    5. Right Words Can Turn An Angry Man Into A Friend, And Wrong Words Can Turn A

Friend Into An Enemy. "A soft answer turneth away wrath: but grievous words stir up anger," (Proverbs 15:1).

6. Your Words Reveal Whether You Are Wise Or A Fool. "The tongue of the wise useth knowledge aright: but the mouth of fools poureth out foolishness," (Proverbs 15:2).

7. Right Words Breathe Life Into Everything Around You. "A wholesome tongue is a tree of life," (Proverbs 15:4).

8. The Purpose of Words Is To Educate, Enthuse And Enlarge Those Around You. "The lips of the wise disperse knowledge," (Proverbs 15:7).

9. Your Personal Happiness Is Influenced By The Words That Come Out of Your Own Mouth. "A man hath joy by the answer of his mouth: and a word spoken in due season, how good is it!" (Proverbs 15:23).

10. The Wise Are Cautious With Their Words. "He that hath knowledge spareth his words," (Proverbs 17:27).

11. Right Words Are As Important As Water On Earth And The Sustaining of Human Life. "The words of a man's mouth are as deep waters, and the wellspring of Wisdom as a flowing brook," (Proverbs 18:4).

12. Men Fail Because of The Words They Speak. "A fool's mouth is his destruction, and his lips are the snare of his soul," (Proverbs 18:7).

13. Wrong Words Wound Others And Destroy People And Friendships Forever. "The words of a talebearer are as wounds, and they go down into the innermost parts of the belly," (Proverbs 18:8).

14. Words Determine Which Dreams Live Or Die. "Death and life are in the power of the tongue: and they that love it shall eat the fruit thereof," (Proverbs 18:21).

15. The Words You Allow Others To Speak Into You Are Deciding The Wisdom You Contain. "Hear counsel, and receive instruction, that thou mayest be wise in thy latter end," (Proverbs 19:20). Solomon knew that words were the difference between his present season and his future season.

16. Wrong Words Are The Reason Men Fall Into Error. "Cease, my son, to hear the instruction that causeth to err from the words of knowledge," (Proverbs 19:27).

17. Good Men Study Their Words Before They Speak Them. "The heart of the righteous studieth to answer," (Proverbs 15:28).

18. The Tongue Is The Major Cause of All Troubles. "Whoso keepeth his mouth and his tongue keepeth his soul from troubles," (Proverbs 21:23).

19. Fools Seldom Understand The Power of Words. "Speak not in the ears of a fool: for he will despise the Wisdom of thy words," (Proverbs 23:9).

20. Talking To Fools Is A Waste of Time. "Speak not in the ears of a fool: for he will despise the Wisdom of thy words," (Proverbs 23:9).

21. Wisdom Is A Result of The Words You Hear. "Hear thou, my son, and be wise," (Proverbs 23:19).

22. The Timing of Your Words Often Decides Your Success Or Failure In A

Situation. "A fool uttereth all his mind: but a wise man keepeth it in till afterwards," (Proverbs 29:11).

23. Influential People Should Use Their Words And Influence To Help The Poor And Needy. "Open thy mouth, judge righteously, and plead the cause of the poor and needy," (Proverbs 31:9).

24. The Words of Wise Women Are Consistently Kind. "She openeth her mouth with Wisdom; and in her tongue is the law of kindness," (Proverbs 31:26).

25. Your Words Can Become The Trap That Destroys You. "Thou art snared with the words of thy mouth," (Proverbs 6:2).

26. Right Words Feed And Sustain Those Around You. "The lips of the righteous feed many: but fools die for want of Wisdom," (Proverbs 10:21).

27. Right Words Are As Important As Silver And Gold. "The tongue of the just is as choice as silver," (Proverbs 10:20).

28. Right Words Can Get You Out of Any Difficulty And Trouble. "The mouth of the upright shall deliver them," (Proverbs 12:6).

29. Right Words Bring Health And Healing. "The tongue of the wise is health," (Proverbs 12:18).

30. The Wise Avoid The Presence of Those Who Consistently Speak Wrong Words. "Go from the presence of a foolish man, when thou perceivest not in him the lips of knowledge," (Proverbs 14:7).

31. Only The Simple And Fools Believe Everything Others Say. "The simple believeth every word: but the prudent man looketh well to his going," (Proverbs 14:15).

32. Right Words Give You Access To Powerful And Important People. "Righteous lips are the delight of kings; and they love him that speaketh right," (Proverbs 16:13).

33. Wisdom Is Necessary In Order To Speak The Right Words. "The heart of the wise teacheth his mouth, and addeth learning to his lips," (Proverbs 16:23).

34. Pleasant Words Are The Sweetest Sounds On Earth. "Pleasant words are as an honeycomb, sweet to the soul, and health to the bones," (Proverbs 16:24).

35. The Sweetness of Right Words Could Help To Cure Any Bitterness Existent In The Human Soul. "Pleasant words are as an honeycomb, sweet to the soul, and health to the bones," (Proverbs 16:24).

36. The Quality of Your Words Reveals The Quality of Your Heart. "An ungodly man diggeth up evil: and in his lips there is as a burning fire," (Proverbs 16:27). You can read the heart of any person by listening to the words they are speaking about others.

37. Words Will Quickly Expose Envy And Jealousy Or Admiration And Respect. "An Ungodly man diggeth up evil: and in his lips there is as a burning fire," (Proverbs 16:27).

38. The Greatest Friendships On Earth Are Broken Because of Wrong Words. "A whisperer separateth chief friends," (Proverbs 16:28).

39. Strife Can Always Be Traced To

Someone's Words. "A froward man soweth strife," (Proverbs 16:28).

40. Evil Is Released Through The Lips. "Moving his lips he bringeth evil to pass," (Proverbs 16:30).

41. You Should Not Answer Anything Until You Have Heard All The Details. "He that answereth a matter before he heareth it, it is folly and shame unto him," (Proverbs 18:13). Accuracy is only important when adequate information is available.

42. Words Influence And Affect The Accumulation of Your Wealth. "A man's belly shall be satisfied with the fruit of his mouth; and with the increase of his lips shall he be filled," (Proverbs 18:20). This is almost never mentioned in prosperity teaching today. Yet using the wrong words can get you fired or prevent you from getting promoted.

I remember times I was going to give someone a raise until I brought them in and heard the words they were speaking. Complaining, blaming, fault-finding words can stop a boss from promoting you.

43. Right Words Can Release A Boss To Promote You Or Give You A Raise. "A man's belly shall be satisfied with the fruit of his mouth; and with the increase of his lips shall he be filled," (Proverbs 18:20).

44. One Conversation With The Wrong Woman Can Destroy Your Life. "The mouth of strange women is a deep pit: he that is abhorred of the Lord shall fall therein," (Proverbs 22:14).

45. Never Enter Into Battle Without

Sufficient Counsel. "For by wise counsel thou shalt make thy war: and in multitude of counsellors there is safety," (Proverbs 24:6).

46. The Wise Avoid "Self-Praise." "Let another man praise thee, and not thine own mouth; a stranger, and not thine own lips," (Proverbs 27:2).

47. Lying Words Can Poison The Attitude of A Boss Toward An Employee. "If a ruler hearken to lies, all his servants are wicked," (Proverbs 29:12).

Use every conversation as a practice moment for improving your speech.

Use Words That Matter In Every Conversation.

This is one of the Secrets of Champions.

RECOMMENDED INVESTMENTS:
Battle Techniques For War Weary Saints (Book/B-07/32 pages/$5)
Seeds of Wisdom on Faith-Talk (Book/B-24/32 pages/$3)

～ 6 ～

INVEST THE TIME NECESSARY TO NEGOTIATE EFFECTIVELY

Negotiate Everything.

I walked into a luggage store here in Dallas many years ago. When I had selected the luggage I desired, I asked the young lady if she could provide a "corporate discount."

"What is a corporate discount?"

"Forty percent off."

"All right!" was her reply.

With one simple question, I saved several hundred dollars. *Negotiate everything.*

While standing at the airline counter, I was informed that my excess baggage was over $200.

"I was hoping you would show me a little mercy today," I joked gently.

The agent thought for a few moments and replied, "All right." With one simple statement, I saved over $200.

Negotiate everything. Your words are creating financial gain or loss.

Your words are bringing Increase or Decrease.

Your words are creating Doors or Walls.

Your words are Bridges or Barricades.

The Scripture teaches it:

"A man shall eat good by the fruit of his mouth," (Proverbs 13:2). "The wicked is snared by the transgression of his lips: but the just shall come out of trouble," (Proverbs 12:13).

Here Are 10 Facts You Should Remember When You Want To Negotiate Successfully

1. **Attend Negotiation Seminars, Listen To Tapes And Secure The Counsel of Qualified Mentors Before Doing Any Serious Negotiation.**

2. **Successful Negotiation Requires The Right Attitude.** Nobody wants to be taken lightly, intimidated or pushed. Everybody is involved. The lady in the luggage store wanted to sell the luggage, create favor and a happy customer. I gave her the information which would accommodate that need, a 40 percent discount. (I later returned to buy many other items because of the favor she showed.)

The airline that graciously permitted me the excess baggage has become my favorite airline receiving over $100,000 of my business each year.

Negotiation must be viewed as a win-win situation for everybody involved.

3. **Successful Negotiation Requires An Understanding of The Cost Involved For Others.** Donald Trump explained why his father was so successful in negotiating prices. His father invested time in finding out exactly what the cost was for those he was negotiating with. This enabled him to know exactly how far to negotiate.

4. **Successful Negotiation Requires Proper Timing.** Many years ago I was very weary

when I arrived home from a meeting. The flight was tiresome. As I walked into the office, a staff member approached me.

"I've got to talk to you!"

"All right. Sit down. How can I help you?"

She was very aggressive and flippant. "I need a raise!"

"Well, how much are you wanting me to increase your salary each month?" I asked.

"I need a $1,000 a month raise."

I almost laughed. I really thought she was joking. She wasn't. She continued, "My husband and I are moving into a new home that we have just built, and I really need the income to pay for the house."

It was ridiculous to me, I almost laughed aloud. But, I proceeded to advise her *gently* that, perhaps, it would be well for her to find another job where she could secure the salary she needed. I asked, "Your present salary was created by a list of problems you chose to solve for me. Now you want a huge increase in salary. Do you have a list of the new problems you will begin to solve for me?"

It had never crossed her mind to solve more problems for her new salary.

5. Successful Negotiation Involves Long-Term Gain, Not Short-Term Gain.

The famous billionaire, Sam Walton, said he never invested in a company for where it would be in 18 months. He invested in companies that would succeed 10 years down the road. An employee can often squeeze out an extra dollar from a boss during a crisis situation. But if it creates a wall of separation, that staff person can cause a deeper problem in the long-term.

6. Successful Negotiation Requires Quality Time. Do not rush anything. You will never do well in something that has not taken thoughtful-ness, sufficient time to collect information and necessary data. Run from the salesman who insists that "this is the last day of this sale." Do not fall for it. When you return a month later, they will still deal! They need your purchase more than they need their own product.

7. Listen Longer To The Needs of Others. Listeners are rare. You are developing an understanding of the concerns, fears and passion of the hearts of those at the negotiating table. Wisdom is worth any price. Invest the time to listen thoroughly, compassionately and expectantly.

8. Successful Negotiation Should Focus On Details That Truly Matter. Several years ago, an impressive young couple wrote me about a job. They were making $5.00 an hour. He was riding a motorcycle to his second job. They had 3 children and worked 16 hours a day on two jobs at $10.00 an hour total. They were destitute. My heart went out to them. They had driven all night to meet me face-to-face for an interview. I agreed to pay him what both his jobs were presently providing for working 16 hours a day. Then, as a gesture of caring, I included their housing if they would do additional yard work at my home. They were thrilled and elated. Over a period of time, I purchased furniture, dishes, clothes and so forth. They were enjoyable, so I was happy to do so.

Soon, someone must have inspired them to negotiate for more. Every opportunity to "squeeze me," such as appliance breakdowns, they pushed. I noticed a pattern. It became one-sided.

When you have many employees, you cannot give everybody a raise when you desire. You cannot always give it to them the moment they deserve it. *You have to think long-term for the organization.* Something within me became agitated. So when the oven broke down, they wanted me to replace it. I was weary of replacing everything. I requested that they pay half, and I would pay the other half. They attempted to use harsh words to negotiate with me. I am not the kind that responds well to intimidation.

I realized they were frustrated. So I explained that they had 45 days to go find a new house, and they could purchase it themselves. Yes, they were good people, but were poor at negotiation. They lost a wonderful blessing trying to squeeze "an extra nickel." Do not lose dollars trying to save pennies.

9. Close Doors Gently. If you realize that you have to end a relationship, close doors quietly. You may have to return through them in the coming years.

10. Never Burn Bridges Behind You. Everybody talks. Everything you do is being discussed by many you have not yet met. Do not schedule unnecessary conflicts in your future.

Yes, I agree, your opinion deserves to be heard.

But make certain that it is heard at the right *time* in the right environment and with the right *attitude.*

Negotiate Everything.

Invest The Time To Negotiate Effectively.

This is one of the Secrets of Champions.

Anyone Who Trivializes
Your Passion Is
An Enemy To Your Dream.

-MIKE MURDOCK

~ 7 ~

TREASURE AND PROTECT YOUR FLOW OF PASSION

Passion Is Desire.

It includes the desire to change, serve or achieve a goal.

Men who succeed greatly possess great passion for their Assignment. They are consumed and obsessed. It burns within them like fire. Nothing else matters to them but the completion of the instructions of God in their lives.

Isaiah was passionate. "For the Lord God will help me; therefore shall I not be confounded: therefore have I set my face like a flint, and I know that I shall not be ashamed," (Isaiah 50:7).

The Apostle Paul was passionate. "Brethren, I count not myself to have apprehended: but this one thing I do, forgetting those things which are behind, and reaching forth unto those things which are before, I press toward the mark for the prize of the high calling of God in Christ Jesus," (Philippians 3:13-14).

Jesus was passionate about completing and finishing His Assignment on earth. "Looking unto Jesus the Author and Finisher of our faith; Who for the joy that was set before Him endured the cross, despising the shame, and is set down at the right hand of the throne of God. For consider Him that endured such contradiction of sinners against Himself, lest ye be wearied and faint in your minds," (Hebrews 12:2-3).

You are instructed to develop a passion for The Word of God. The Lord spoke to Joshua about the Law and instructed him to "turn not from it to the right hand or to the left, that thou mayest prosper whithersoever thou goest. This book of the law shall not depart out of thy mouth; but thou shalt meditate therein day and night, that thou mayest observe to do according to all that is written therein: for then thou shalt make thy way prosperous, and then thou shalt have good success," (Joshua 1:7-8).

So, move toward His presence today. Habitually schedule time in The Secret Place. "He that dwelleth in The Secret Place of the most High shall abide under the shadow of the Almighty," (Psalm 91:1). In His presence, your passion for Him will grow from a tiny acorn to a huge oak within you.

Wrong relationships will weaken your passion for your Assignment for God. Recently, I went to dinner with several friends after a service. Within one hour, the discussion had become filled with the problems with people, financial difficulties and complaining attitudes. I was shocked at what began to grow within me. Though I had left the service with great joy, something began to die within me. As others discussed the difficult situations in their lives or how difficult it was to reach their goals, I felt my own fire begin to go out. Paul warned of such associations. "Be not deceived: evil communications corrupt good manners," (1 Corinthians 15:33).

Protect the Gift of Passion within you. Guard your focus every hour. Be ruthless with distractions. Feed the picture of your goal continually. Watch for the Four Enemies of Passion: fatigue, busyness, over-scheduling and putting God last on your daily schedule.

Passion Is Power.

You will never have significant success with anything *until it becomes an obsession with you.* An obsession is when something consumes your thoughts and time.

You will only be remembered in life for your obsession. Henry Ford, the automobile. Thomas Edison, inventions. Billy Graham, evangelism. Oral Roberts, healing. The Wright Brothers, the airplane.

Jesus had a passion for His mission and goal in life. "For the Son of man is come to seek and to save that which was lost," (Luke 19:10). "How God anointed Jesus of Nazareth with the Holy Ghost and with power: Who went about doing good, and healing all that were oppressed of the devil; for God was with Him," (Acts 10:38).

Jesus focused on doing the exact instructions of His Heavenly Father. He healed the sick. He noticed the lonely. He came to make people successful, to restore and repair their life to full fellowship with His Father.

You Will Only Have Significant Success With Something That Is An Obsession.

That obsession took Him to the cross. It took Him to the crucifixion. Eight inches of thorns were crushed into His Brow. A spear punctured His side. Spikes were driven into His hands. Thirty-nine stripes of a whip tore His back to shreds. Four hundred soldiers spit on His body. His beard was ripped off His face. But He was *obsessed with the salvation of mankind.*

And He succeeded.

You may start small. You may start with very little. But, if what you love begins to consume your mind, your thoughts, your conversation, your schedule, look for extraordinary success.

Do you dread going to work every morning? Do you anxiously look at the clock toward closing time each afternoon? Is your mind wandering throughout the day toward other places or things you would love to be doing? Then you will probably not have much success at what you are doing.

Find something that consumes you. Something that is worthy of building your entire life around. Consider it.

An Uncommon Assignment Will Require Uncommon Passion.

Treasure And Protect Your Flow of Passion.

This is one of the Secrets of Champions.

☜ 8 ☞

BE WILLING TO START SMALL

———⟫➋–O–❮⟪———

Little Things Matter.

Small hinges control huge doors. Small keys unlock vaults containing millions of dollars. A little steering determines the direction of a huge semi-truck. One small finger dialing the telephone can start a business transaction of one billion dollars. *Never despise small beginnings.* "For who hath despised the day of small things?" (Zechariah 4:10).

Many will never achieve a great Assignment because they want their beginning to be spectacular. I am reminded of the fascinating story of Naaman, the captain of the host of the king of Syria. He was a leper. When he went to the house of Elisha, the prophet sent him a simple instruction. Elisha sent a message to him to go and wash in the Jordan River seven times. Naaman was infuriated. He had a different mental picture of how his healing would occur. One of his servants made an interesting statement, "My father, if the prophet had bid thee do some great thing, wouldest thou not have done it? How much rather then, when he saith to thee, Wash, and be clean?" (2 Kings 5:13).

The Assignment from Elisha was simple, clear and direct. Naaman was to go wash in Jordan 7 times.

When You Do The Simple, The Supernatural Occurs.

Small Beginnings Often Have Great Endings.

Jesus understood this principle. He was born in a stable. His beginning was in a small town of Bethlehem. It did not matter to Him, because He knew His destiny. He was aware of the greatness of His *destination.* One of His greatest statements ever is, "He that is faithful in that which is least is faithful also in much: and he that is unjust in the least is unjust also in much," (Luke 16:10).

Attention To Details Produces Excellence. It is the difference between extraordinary champions and losers. So, do not despise and feel insignificant in your small acts of obedience while giving birth to your Assignment.

One of the great evangelists of our day began his ministry duplicating tapes for his mentor. Hour after hour, day after day, he sat and duplicated tapes. He listened to each tape over and over. He served. He ministered. He assisted. It was the *beginning* of a significant ministry.

Ruth began as an ignorant Moabite heathen girl. Her attention to the small details of her Assignment, Naomi, positioned her as the great-grandmother of David and ushered in the lineage of Jesus.

Abigail brought lunch to the starving man, David. She became his wife.

When Jesus Wanted To Produce A Great Miracle, He Always Gave A Small Instruction.

Little things mattered to Him. Notice the small

insignificant instructions that Jesus gave. They almost seemed ridiculous. Some might think these were instructions given to children, but none of them were. Rather, they were given to grown men, to mature adults.

"Go wash in the pool of Siloam," (John 9:7). A big miracle. Yes, a blind man was healed from a lifetime of blindness.

"Launch out into the deep, and let down your nets for a draught," (Luke 5:4). This small instruction produced the *greatest catch of fish the disciples had ever gathered.*

"Fill the waterpots with water," (John 2:7). It produced the *greatest wine* anyone had ever tasted, ever. It happened at the marriage of Canaan.

"Arise, and take up thy bed, and go thy way into thine house," (Mark 2:11). What was the result? A man sick of the palsy, *immediately arose,* took up his bed, and went forth before them all and many glorified God because of it.

"Bring them hither to Me," (Matthew 14:18). These words were spoken regarding the 5 loaves and 2 fishes, the lunch of a lad. What happened afterwards has been preached around the world. *Thousands were fed miraculously,* and at the conclusion, each of the 12 disciples had a basketful to bring home!

▶ Great miracles do not require great instructions.

▶ Great miracles require *obeyed* instructions.

A student in Bible school sits in chapel daily awaiting a neon sign in the Heavens declaring, "Bob, go to Calcutta, India." It never happens. Why? Bob has not obeyed the *first* instruction. "Bob, go to the prayer room at 7:00 a.m."

Obedience Turns A Common Instruction Into An Uncommon Miracle.

God does not give great instructions to great men.

God Gives Uncommon Instructions To Common Men. But when you obey that instruction, greatness is birthed. "If ye be willing and obedient, ye shall eat the good of the land," (Isaiah 1:19).

Nothing you will do today is small in the eyes of God.

Your Assignment May Have Small Beginnings.

Be Willing To Start Small.

This is one of the Secrets of Champions.

RECOMMENDED INVESTMENTS:
The Law of Recognition (Book/B-114/247 pages/$15)
7 Signposts to Your Assignment (Book/B-122/32 pages/$7)
7 Power Keys To Getting What You Want (Book/B-127/32 pages/$7)

❧ 9 ❧

VIEW YOURSELF AS A PROBLEM-SOLVER

You Are Here For A Reason.

To assign means to set apart or mark for a specific purpose. "But know that the Lord hath set apart him that is godly for Himself," (Psalm 4:3).

The Bible, The Manufacturer's Handbook, is filled with examples of those who discovered and embraced their Assignment.

► *Moses* solved problems for the *Israelites*.
► *Aaron* solved problems for *Moses*.
► *Jonathan* was assigned to *David*.
► *Jonah* was assigned to the *Ninevites*.
► A *Handmaiden* helped *Naaman* get healed.
► *Ruth* was assigned to *Naomi*.

You, too, are assigned to solve problems.

For somebody.

Somewhere.

You are the *Healer* for someone sick.

You are the *Life Jacket* for someone drowning.

You are the *Ruler* over someone unruly.

You are the *Lifter* for someone fallen.

You have asked these questions a thousand times. Why am I here? Why *me?* What is my *purpose?* Is there *really* a God? Where did I come from? Did I exist in another world before this one?

A poem is the proof of a *poet.*

A song is the proof of a *composer.*

A product is the proof of a *manufacturer.*

Creation is the proof of the *Creator.*

Why were you born? It is an excellent question. It is a wonderful question. It is a frequent question. It is an *answerable* question. You deserve an answer. The answer exists. The answers are clear. The answers are more obvious than many realize.

The Manufacturer is God.

The Product is You.

The Manual is the Bible.

- ▶ You were created to bring pleasure to God. (See Revelation 4:11.)
- ▶ You have been set apart for an exclusive purpose and reason. "But know that the Lord hath set apart him that is godly for Himself," (Psalm 4:3).
- ▶ You will give an account of your conduct and productivity. "So then every one of us shall give account of himself to God," (Romans 14:12).

Every product contains more answers than we first realized. Study the car. The fact that it *moves* is proof that it has a different *purpose* than your home. Compare a baseball bat and a sandwich. The hardness of one and the softness of the other is an obvious *clue* that their purpose *differs.*

Studying your difference rather than your similarity to others will produce an incredible revelation of Wisdom. Especially regarding your Assignment—the problem you were created to solve.

Mechanics solve car problems.

Lawyers solve legal problems.

Ministers solve spiritual problems.

I had an interesting experience during a recent telephone conversation. While talking to someone very important in my life, I realized suddenly that I was merely listening. In fact, they asked me nothing. He did not ask me for my opinion, or feelings or observations. I waited patiently. Then, I thought, "Why am I even listening to this when he obviously does not want solutions or he would ask me questions?" Then it dawned on me. My *listening* was his solution. He simply needed someone to listen to his pain, discomfort and heartache. Yes, even listening to someone hurting near you is often a marvelous therapy and solution to their problem.

Motivational speakers receive thousands of dollars to solve a problem for salesmen in a company. Effective counselors make an excellent living simply by being willing to listen patiently, thoughtfully and consistently to their clients.

Sometimes *words* heal.

Sometimes *silence* heals.

Sometimes *listening* heals.

It is important that you recognize your Assignment. It is essential that you embrace the *difference* in your Assignment. It is important that you are willing to be mentored for it.

Your function is *different* from others.

The *function* of others is different from yours.

Counselors provide *answers* to problems.

Comedians provide *escape* from problems.

Your Assignment is always to someone with a problem. Do not run from it. Embrace it.

9 Exciting Benefits of Problems

1.   **Problems Are The Gates To Your Significance.**
2.   **Problems Are Wonderful, Glorious Seeds For Change.**
3.   **Problems Link You To Others.**
4.   **Problems Provide Your Income.**
5.   **Problems Birth Opportunity To Reveal Your Uniqueness.**
6.   **Problems Birth New Relationships.**
7.   **Problems Are The Real Reason Friendships Exist.**
8.   **Remove Problems From The Earth, And You Will Destroy Any Sense of Significance In Humanity.**
9.   **Problems Bring Good People Together During Bad Times.**

The mechanic knows that an automobile problem is his connection to you.

The lawyer knows that a legal problem is his connection to you.

The dentist knows that a tooth problem is his connection to you.

The Problem God Created You To Solve On Earth Is Called Your Assignment.

View Yourself As A Problem-Solver.

This is one of the Secrets of Champions.

❧ 10 ❧

STAY IN YOUR CENTER OF EXPERTISE

━━━━━━▶❂◀━━━━━━

Do What You Do Best.

What do you *love* to do? What do you *love* to talk about? What would you rather *hear* about than anything else on earth? What would you do with your life *if money was not a factor?* What would you do *best* of all?

Your joy is determined by doing what you love.

Jesus associated with fishermen. He talked to tax collectors. Doctors and lawyers and religious leaders were regularly in His life. *But He never wavered from His focus.* "How God anointed Jesus of Nazareth with the Holy Ghost and with power: Who went about doing good, and healing all that were oppressed of the devil; for God was with Him," (Acts 10:38).

He knew His mission.

He stayed focused. I really believe that *broken focus is the reason men fail.*

Some people take jobs because they are convenient or close to their home. One man told me that he had spent his entire life working on a job that made him miserable.

"Why have you worked there for 27 years then?"

I asked.

"It is only 10 minutes from my house," he replied. "And in 3 years I will receive a gold watch. I do not want to leave too early and miss my gold watch."

What you love is a clue to your calling and talent. Stay In Your Center of Expertise.

This is one of the Secrets of Champions.

RECOMMENDED INVESTMENTS:
Wisdom For Winning (Book/B-01/228 pages/$10)
Finding Your Purpose In Life (Book/B-05/32 pages/$5)
The Mentor's Manna on Abilities (Book/B-73/32 pages/$3)

❧ 11 ❧

DELEGATE ANYTHING
ANOTHER CAN DO

―――――❧⬩❍⬩❧―――――

Know Your Limitations.

It is more productive to set 10 men to work rather than you do the work of 10 men. *Delegation is simply giving others necessary instructions and motivation to complete a particular task.* This takes time. It takes patience. But it is a long-term benefit.

Jesus commanded the multitudes. He instructed His disciples to have the people sit down. He distributed the loaves and fishes to His disciples for distribution. (See Matthew 14:19.)

Jesus sent His disciples to get a donkey. (See Matthew 21:2.)

Jesus gave instructions to a blind man to complete his healing. (See John 9:6-7.)

Jesus sent His disciples into cities to prepare for special meals. (See Mark 14:12-15.)

The early church leaders understood the importance of delegating.

"And in those days, when the number of the disciples was multiplied, there arose a murmuring of the Grecians against the Hebrews, because their widows were neglected in the daily ministration. Then the 12 called the multitude of the disciples unto them, and said, It is not reason that we should leave the word of God, and serve tables. Wherefore, brethren, look ye out among you seven men of honest report, full of the Holy Ghost and Wisdom, whom we may appoint over this business. But we will give ourselves continually to prayer, and to the ministry of the word," (Acts 6:1-4).

5 Important Things You Need To Remember When You Network With Others

1.   **Make A Checklist of Their Specific Responsibilities.**

2.   **Carefully Instruct Them As To Your Total Expectations of Them.**

3.   **Give Them The Information And Authority Necessary To Complete Those Tasks.**

4.   **Set A Specific Deadline To Finish The Task.**

5.   **Clearly Show Them How They Will Be Rewarded For Their Effort.**

Take time to motivate and educate those you work with so they know exactly what you expect. *Take the time to delegate.*

Delegate Anything Another Can Do.

This is one of the Secrets of Champions.

RECOMMENDED INVESTMENTS:
The Leadership Secrets of Jesus (Book/B-91/196 pages/$12)
Secrets of the Richest Man Who Ever Lived (Book/B-99/
   179 pages/$12)
Seeds of Wisdom on Productivity (Book/B-137/32 pages/$5)

∽ 12 ∽

TREASURE GOLDEN CONNECTIONS

Friendship Deserves Care And Attention.
Successful people treasure worthy friendships. Names are vital. Building a significant rolodex or address book is a *must*. Keep in touch regularly with those who love you.

Every successful pastor knows the importance of a name. That's why visitor cards are given out at most services. Receptions where greeters meet newcomers are held every Sunday morning. Millions of dollars are spent on television programs, radio broadcasts and newspaper ads—because of the name of those who are important to their vision.

Every successful businessman knows the importance of a single name. Listen to Ron Popeil, a multimillionaire who has enjoyed great success. "One of the mandates at Ronco, besides quality and innovation, is this: A name, address and phone number are worth gold. We always capture a telephone number in addition to the name and address of a customer, because those items are very common, very valuable," (page 219, *The Salesman of the Century*).

Avoid keeping names and addresses in many different places.

Keep one Master Address Book.

I call mine, "The Problem-Solvers."

My dentist's name is kept under "D." When I want to buy carpet, I look under "C" where I have placed the business card of a local carpet store.

Think of everyone around you as a potential problem-solver for your life. Treasure your access to them. When you receive a business card, place it under the divider most appropriate. For instance, if you meet Mr. Sam Jones who sells automobiles, do not put his business card under "J" for Jones. You will not remember it a year later. Place his business card under "A" for automobiles.

Friendships are too precious to lose. They cost too much to treat lightly. I once read where one of our U.S. presidents had 7,500 names in his rolodex. He loved people. He valued people. He knew the importance of a name.

Build a Master Address Book of those who truly matter to your life.

Treasure Golden Connections.

This is one of the Secrets of Champions.

RECOMMENDED INVESTMENTS:
Seeds of Wisdom on Relationships (Book/B-14/32 pages/$3)
The Double Diamond Principle (Book/B-39/148 pages/$9)
7 Signposts to Your Assignment (Book/B-122/32 pages/$7)

❧ 13 ❧

IDENTIFY TIME-WASTERS

Your Daily Agenda Is Your Life.
You cannot save time. You cannot collect it. You cannot place it in a special bank vault. You are only permitted to *spend* it, wisely or foolishly. *You must do something with time.*

You will invest it or you will waste it.

Everyone has a hidden agenda. Those around you will be reaching to pull you "off course." You must be careful to *protect your list of priorities.*

Jesus did. There is a fascinating story in the Bible about it.

Lazarus, a close friend of Jesus, became sick. Mary and Martha, his two sisters, sent word to Jesus to come. However, "When He had heard therefore that he was sick, He abode two days still in the same place where He was," (John 11:6). Mary was upset, "Lord, if thou hadst been here, my brother had not died," (John 11:21).

But Jesus had deliberately delayed His coming. He kept His own schedule. He protected His agenda. He did not allow the emergencies of others to get him off track. *He guarded His list of priorities.*

Only You Know Your Priorities.

Make today count. Remember the 24 golden box cars on the track of success. If you do not control what goes into each of your 24 golden box cars (hours), then somebody else will.

Avoid distractions. Write your daily list of things to do. Protect your schedule. *This is your life.* Make it happen.

Identify Time-Wasters.

This is one of the Secrets of Champions.

RECOMMENDED INVESTMENTS:
Seeds of Wisdom on Relationships (Book/B-14/32 pages/$3)
Seven Obstacles To Abundant Success (Book/B-64/32 pages/$5)
The Assignment: The Anointing & The Adversity, Volume 2 (Book/
B-75/192 pages/$12)

≈ 14 ≈

Ask Quality Questions Continually

━━━━━━━━━⟫⊙⟪━━━━━

Ask Questions.

"Hear counsel, and receive instruction, that thou mayest be wise in thy latter end," (Proverbs 19:20).

Ask questions to accurately determine the needs and desires of others.

Interrogate your world. Insist on listening to the opinions and needs of others.

Almost nobody on earth listens to others, nor questions them.

It is a master secret of success.

Jesus asked questions.

Once Simon Peter went fishing. He caught nothing. When the morning was come, Jesus was standing on the shore. Jesus calls out, "Children, have ye any meat?" (John 21:5). *He assumed nothing. He pursued information.*

Their answer was His entry point into their life. He had something they needed. *He had information.*

His question was a link to their future. *It was the bridge for their relationship.* He then instructed them, "Cast the net on the right side of the ship, and ye shall find," (John 21:6).

Information Is The Difference Between Your Present And Your Future.

Document the needs of others. Keep a Rolodex. Keep a notebook of their needs and desires. What are your customers' needs today? Are you *really listening* to them? Do they really feel you are listening to them? Most employees feel that their bosses really do not hear their complaints. Most employers feel that their employees do not interpret them correctly.

Jesus pursued information.

Ask Quality Questions Continually.

This is one of the Secrets of Champions.

 Our Prayer Together...
"Father, open my eyes and ears to correctly see and hear information. Constantly remind me of the importance of information and how it can determine my success. In Jesus' Name. Amen."

RECOMMENDED INVESTMENTS:
Thirty-One Secrets of an Unforgettable Woman (Book/B-57/
  140 pages/$12)
Wisdom—God's Golden Key To Success (Book/B-71/67 pages/$7)
31 Secrets of The Uncommon Mentor (6 Tapes/TS-37/$30)

≈ 15 ≈

NETWORK WITH PEOPLE OF ALL BACKGROUNDS

Greatness Is Everywhere.

"The heart of the prudent getteth knowledge; and the ear of the wise seeketh knowledge," (Proverbs 18:15).

People have different contributions. I believe you need different kinds of input into your life. Someone needs what you possess. You need something that they can contribute to you. You are the sum total of your experiences.

Personalities differ. Each person around you contains a different body of knowledge. It is up to you to "drop your pail in their well," and draw it out. "Where no counsel is, the people fall: but in the multitude of counsellors there is safety," (Proverbs 11:14).

Look at those who surrounded Jesus. A tax collector. A physician. A fisherman. A woman who had been possessed with seven devils.

Some were poor. Some were wealthy. Some were very energetic while others were passive. Some were explosive like Peter. Others, like James, were logical.

Be willing to listen to others. Everyone sees through different eyes. They feel with different hearts. They hear through different ears. *Someone knows something that you should know.* You will not discover it until you take the time to stop and hear them out. *One piece of information can turn a failure into a success.* Great decisions are products of great thoughts.

Pay Any Price To Stay In The Presence of Extraordinary People.

Jesus networked.

Network With People of All Backgrounds.

This is one of the Secrets of Champions.

Our Prayer Together...

"I realize, Lord, that Your creation is filled with many extraordinary and different people. Give me the Wisdom and ability to recognize that who I spend my time with is time invested in my success. In Jesus' Name, I rely upon You as my source. Amen."

RECOMMENDED INVESTMENTS:
The Jesus Book (Book/B-27/166 pages/$10)
Thirty-One Secrets of an Unforgettable Woman (Book/B-57/
   140 pages/$12)
Secrets of the Richest Man Who Ever Lived (Book/B-99/
   179 pages/$12)

⇜ 16 ⇝

ALLOW YOURSELF TIME TO CHANGE

━━━━━━⟊-○-⟊━━━━━━

Do Not Be Too Hard On Yourself.

Little-by-little and day-by-day, you will start tasting the rewards of change.

Look at the patience of God with Israel. He "knew they were but flesh." He took many years to even train their leader, Moses. You are not an exception.

Every man fails. Champions simply get back up...and begin again.

Give God time to work.

Sometimes those things you desire the most may take longer to achieve. It takes longer to make a Rolls Royce automobile than a bicycle.

Millions of Miracles have been dashed on the Rocks of Impatience. Give God time.

Something good is happening that you do not see. Wait joyfully with great expectation.

"The Lord upholdeth all that fall, and raiseth up all those that be bowed down," (Psalm 145:14).

"And let us not be weary in well doing: for in due season we shall reap, if we faint not," (Galatians 6:9).

Allow Yourself Time To Change.

This is one of the Secrets of Champions.

What You Can Tolerate,
You Cannot Change.

-MIKE MURDOCK

～ 17 ～

ABANDON ABUSIVE RELATIONSHIPS

There Are 4 Kinds of People In Your Life: Those Who Add, Subtract, Divide And Multiply.

Those Who Do Not Increase You, Will Inevitably Decrease You.

It is the responsibility of others to discern your worth.

A contentious person is a trouble-maker. He spreads discontent, frustration and distrust.

He gossips. He slanders. He promotes strife.

Do not feed a relationship with such a person.

"Make no friendship with an angry man; and with a furious man thou shalt not go: Lest thou learn his ways, and get a snare to thy soul," (Proverbs 22:24-25).

"As coals are to burning coals, and wood to fire; so is a contentious man to kindle strife," (Proverbs 26:21).

Abandon Abusive Relationships.

This is one of the Secrets of Champions.

RECOMMENDED INVESTMENTS:
Seeds of Wisdom on Relationships (Book/B-14/32 pages/$3)
Seeds of Wisdom on Warfare (Book/B-19/32 pages/$3)

You Can Only Be Promoted
By The Person
Whose Instruction You
Have Followed.

-MIKE MURDOCK

~ 18 ~

EMBRACE THE CORRECTION OF UNCOMMON ACHIEVERS

God Assigns Deliverers.

Moses was assigned to lead the Israelites out of Egypt. Elijah was sent to the widow of Zarephath to help her use her faith.

If you are sick, look for the man of God who believes in healing. If you are having financial problems, look for the man of God who believes in prosperity. No one fails alone. If you fail, it will be because you chose to ignore those God assigned to help you.

Recognize messengers from God. When satan wants to destroy you, he sends a person. *When God wants to bless you, He sends a person.* Recognize them. Whether they are packaged like a John the Baptist in a loincloth of camel's hair, or the silk robes of King Solomon.

Your reaction to a man or woman of God is carefully documented by God. When God talks to you, it is often through the spiritual leaders in your life. Do not ignore them.

"He that receiveth a prophet in the name of a

prophet shall receive a prophet's reward: and he that receiveth a righteous man in the name of a righteous man shall receive a righteous man's reward," (Matthew 10:41).

Embrace The Correction of Uncommon Achievers.

This is one of the Secrets of Champions.

⚌ 19 ⚌

DECIDE THE LEGACY YOU
WANT TO LEAVE

You Will Only Succeed With Something That Consumes You.

Significant achievers build their *daily agenda* around *their Assignment.* Their schedule and their plan is totally focused on the completion of their Assignment. Their library is filled with books... about their Assignment. Their best friends are those who *celebrate* (not tolerate) *their Assignment.*

When you hear the name of Thomas Edison, you think of inventions. When you hear the name of Oral Roberts, you think of healing. When you hear the name of Henry Ford, you think of an automobile. When you hear the name of Michael Jordan, you think of basketball.

You Will Only Be Remembered For Your Obsession In Life. It may be a good one or an evil one. Whether you are Billy Graham or Adolph Hitler—you will be known for one thing: *What consumes you,* your mind and your time.

Ruth would not even pursue the normal path of dating others. She built her lifestyle around the survival of Naomi. *She never considered an option.*

It may be your personal *business.* It may be the spiritual life of your *children. You will almost always succeed with anything that has the ability to demand your total focus and attention.*

Joshua called it "not looking to the right or to the left." Others call it being single-minded. "A double minded man is unstable in all his ways," (James 1:8).

She refused to consider any alternatives to her Assignment. Ruth would not go back to her family. She refused to return to the village of her youth. She had developed total focus on her Assignment.

The Only Reason Men Fail Is Broken Focus. If you fail in life...it will be because something was introduced to you as an option, an alternative to what God told you to do with your life, and *you accepted it.*

Look at Moses. "When he was come to years, refused to be called the son of Pharaoh's daughter; Choosing rather to suffer affliction with the people of God, than to enjoy pleasures of sin for a season; Esteeming the reproach of Christ greater riches than the treasures in Egypt: for he had respect unto the recompence of the reward," (Hebrews 11:24-26).

There is no Plan B for your life. There is only one plan. It is the master plan of the Creator Who made you. Consider nothing else as an option.

That is what made Ruth an unforgettable woman. As Naomi walked with her two daughters-in-law, Orpah and Ruth, she turned and said, "Go, return each to her mother's house: the Lord deal kindly with you, as ye have dealt with the dead, and with me. The Lord grant you that ye may find rest, each of you in the house of her husband," (Ruth 1:8-9). She kissed them. They wept.

Both said, "We will return with thee unto thy people."

Naomi instructed, "Turn again, my daughters: why will ye go with me? are there yet any more sons in my womb, that they may be your husbands? Turn again, my daughters, go your way; for I am too old to have an husband," (Ruth 1:11-12).

They lifted up their voice.

They wept again.

Orpah left.

But Ruth cleaved unto her.

Naomi rebukes, "Behold thy sister in law is gone back unto her people, and unto her gods: return thou after thy sister in law," (Ruth 1:15).

Ruth is *tenacious.*

She is *bold.*

She is *focused.*

Her husband is dead.

Her father-in-law is dead.

Her sister-in-law has returned to her family.

Her mother-in-law is instructing her to return home.

There is not one encourager in her circle. She does not have one single spiritual cheerleader in her life.

She is *alone.*

She is the only one with the desire to pursue a different future.

Her past has no encouraging memories.

Her present has no encouraging motivation.

Her future is up to her alone.

She knows it.

"Intreat me not to leave thee, or to return from

following after thee: for whither thou goest, I will go; and where thou lodgest, I will lodge; thy people shall be my people, and thy God my God: Where thou diest, will I die, and there will I be buried: the Lord do so to me, and more also, if ought but death part thee and me," (Ruth 1:16-17).

She was willing to motivate herself when nobody else was capable or caring.

Most of us appreciate a lot of encouragement. Daily. Consistently. It is wonderful when your mate is there to hold your hand through the valleys of uncertainty. It is a precious thing when your little girl looks up and says, "Daddy, you can do anything!"

Your pastor is a gift from the Lord when he looks into your eyes and tells you, "I prayed for you last night, and God spoke to me to reassure you and tell you that your circumstances are going to change very soon."

But what if there were no one in your life to speak a word to encourage you? Would you still persist in the way you are going? Would you stay focused? Would you remain bold and tenacious in your goal and dream—when absolutely nobody really cared?

That is what made Ruth an unforgettable woman.

It is what can make you an unforgettable champion right now.

You see, *every true champion knows seasons of aloneness.* Moses must have known *seasons of insignificance* alone in the desert. David must have felt disconnected from the great climate his brothers enjoyed, as they won victory after victory in Saul's army. Certainly, it is wonderful and desirable to have encouragement around you. But if you are really going to produce significantly, you must learn the secret of *motivating yourself...encouraging yourself*...accessing the deepest currents within your own heart.

If you keep waiting for everyone else—you will never move from where you are.

You can *stay* motivated.

You can *stay* enthusiastic.

You can *stay* energized.

You can motivate yourself—when you develop a consuming obsession for a specific future you desire.

So stop complaining that your mate is not interested in your personal dreams.

Stop whining when your children show no interest in your personal goals.

Stop holding self-pity parties. Nobody attends them anyhow.

Embrace your future. Do it with total abandonment, joy and full excitement that *tomorrow is going to be the best season of your life.*

Decide The Legacy You Want To Leave.

This is one of the Secrets of Champions.

RECOMMENDED INVESTMENTS:

Thirty-One Secrets of an Unforgettable Woman (Book/B-57/ 140 pages/$12)

The Assignment: The Dream & The Destiny (Book/B-74/ 164 pages/$12)

The Assignment: The Anointing & The Adversity (Book/B-75/ 192 pages/$12)

The Assignment: The Trials & The Triumphs (Book/B-97/ 160 pages/$12)

The Assignment: The Pain & The Passion (Book/B-98/ 144 pages/$12)

The Atmosphere You Create Determines The Product You Produce.

-MIKE MURDOCK

≈ 20 ≈

CREATE THE ENVIRONMENT THAT KEEPS YOU STIMULATED

Atmosphere Matters.

Invest whatever is necessary to create the atmosphere that motivates you.

Your chosen focus requires a unique climate.

Your surroundings are so important. Your atmosphere must receive your attention. It will not happen automatically. You must control the atmosphere around your life or it will control you.

16 Keys In Creating The Climate And Atmosphere You Need

1. Your Climate Influences The Decisions You Make. When you are in a high fashion clothing store, the music is often quiet, classical or dignified. When you go into a store where the younger generation makes purchases, the music is fast, upbeat and energizing. The merchants have created an environment that influences you to buy.

2. Your Surroundings Contain Colors That Affect You Emotionally. Many years ago, I read where a certain shade of pink was used in prisons to reduce violence and fights. Some say that bodybuilders can lose one third of their ability if they look at a pink wall while working out. Colors affect us. Colors affect our strength, our enthusiasm and the decisions we make.

3. **Everyone Needs Something Different Around Them.** You must discern what environment and atmosphere brings out the best in you.

When I need energy and must move quickly from project to project, I love to listen to praise music that is *energizing* and exciting. When I want to ponder and reflect, I love to listen to slower, more worshipful music. I know the value of *protecting the climate* around myself.

4. **Nobody Else Can Create Your Atmosphere For You.** You must discern it and pursue it for yourself.

5. **Nobody Else Really Cares About Your Specific Needs Like You Do.** So, do not wait and hope someone emerges who will take an aggressive part in making it happen for you.

6. **Nobody Else Is Responsible For Providing You With The Climate You Desire.** It is *your* life, *your* needs and *your* decisions.

7. **You Will Not Do Your Very Best Until Everything Around You Is In Place.** Yes, you may achieve and be productive to a degree. But, you can multiply the results of your life when the things *around* you strengthen and motivate you.

8. **What You See Controls What You Desire.** When you see a billboard advertising hamburgers, you suddenly receive a desire for hamburgers. That's why you must put around yourself pictures and images of the things you want.

9. **What You Are Viewing Daily Affects**

What You Desire To Do. When children see the playground at McDonald's, they are suddenly inspired to stop everything and go play.

10. Keep Around You Photographs of Things You Want In Your Future. It may be a boat you want to buy, a home you want to live in or a picture of yourself 20 pounds lighter. These images are influencing *the direction* your decisions will take you.

11. Your Environment Is Worth Any Investment In Music And Equipment. Buy a stereo or whatever it takes—get the *best* possible.

Every morning, I listen to the Scriptures on cassette tape. That's the first thing I do each day. Yes, they cost. The cassette recorder costs. But, my future and my emotions are worth any investment.

I purchase candles that smell the best, strongest and last the longest. Placing them around my room helps provide the most incredible atmosphere of reflection, warmth and caring. I need that. My heart requires it. If I do not do it, it will not be done. So, because it is my life that is so vital to me, I invest *whatever is necessary.*

A few days ago, I spent over $100 on several CDs. Yet, when I purchased them, I really was not just purchasing some music on compact discs. *I was purchasing an atmosphere.*

You see, this morning, after listening to the Bible on tape, I turned the CD player on. On the 6 CDs were birds, a sparkling, flowing fountain and peaceful music. Within seconds, I felt like I was under the trees alone and quiet, tasting the richness of God's nature around me. Yet, I was in my *bedroom!* I did not have to spend $2,000 to take a vacation to Honolulu. I simply needed an investment in my atmosphere—the appropriate CDs.

12. Your Investment In Interior Decorating Can Make A Huge Difference In Your Productivity. A new rug, a picture on the wall, a vase with a rose, every small thing can increase the warmth and caring of your environment.

13. Invest The Effort And Experimentation To Discover What You Really Need Around You. That is all right, too. It is wonderful to explore variations of climates and environments. An interior decorator, the suggestions of a friend or your own personal visits to different stores can help you discover the atmosphere you prefer to work in, play around or simply relax and rest in. Each atmosphere produces a different emotion.

14. Do Not Wait On Others To Initiate Changes In Your Environment. Make any investment necessary to create the kind of environment that inspires you toward excellence and the improvement of your life.

15. Your Atmosphere Can Often Determine Your Productivity. Many businesses have discovered an increase in unity and employee morale when they played music quietly throughout their offices.

16. What You See Affects The Decisions You Are Making. It does not cost you a fortune to create a favorable atmosphere. Just think, look around and ask questions. Explore a little. Experiment.

Create The Environment That Keeps You Stimulated.

It is one of the Secrets of Champions.

≈ 21 ≈

DISTINGUISH BETWEEN WHAT MATTERS AND WHAT DOESN'T

Be Decisive.

Ruth was *decisive.* Few people are.

Have you ever noticed the hesitation in car drivers at a 4 way stop? I have seen people sit for 30 seconds at a 4 way stop waiting for everyone else to make the first move! I have sat at restaurants with people who could not decide in 20 minutes what food they wanted to eat! Some have even asked the waitress what *she* thought they should eat!

Develop decisiveness. Think about what you want. Give it thought. Invest the Seed of time. Contemplate. *Meditate on it.*

What do you want to be happening in the circle of your life *10 years from today?* What are the *ideal* circumstances for your retirement? *What do you dream of becoming?* Do you have a personal list of goals and dreams? Have you taken the time to *write them out in detail?*

Several years ago a brilliant young lady suggested that I take a tape recorder, walk into each room of my home and describe clearly what I wished that room to look like. Something wonderful happened! I described exactly how many pens and pencils I wanted, the kind of paper I wanted beside the telephone, and so forth. It became elaborate, energizing and thrilling.

Few people have taken the time to find out what really excites them, energizes them and motivates them.

Something interesting happened in my personal meditation time some weeks ago. I had been a little concerned that my interests frequently changed. For example, the colors my decorator would select for my home would be exciting and thrilling to me. I felt that I would never want to change my mind about them for years to come. A few weeks later, I discovered another combination of colors that excited me again. Obviously, I did not feel comfortable about suddenly changing everything that had been done in my home. Nor did I really have the finances to do so. I bought a car. Loved it...for about 3 weeks. Then, I was bored and wanted a change.

I felt impressed of The Holy Spirit to begin to write down a list of things that had *never changed* inside me over many years. It was quite a list of interesting things...and it really put my mind at ease that there was more stability within me than I realized. Many things have *never* changed whatsoever within me, such as my love for information, my desire to collect books and my excitement over receiving a rare new coin from a friend. Another thing that has never changed is my continual need to change my environment. Regardless of how beautifully my bedroom or kitchen were done...within 12 months or so, I was tired of it. That has been consistent.

Some things never change about you. What are

they? Put down this book for about 15 minutes. Take a sheet of paper, and as quickly and thoroughly as possible, begin to document the things about yourself that have been pretty consistent over the years. Go ahead. Do it now.

Now, after you have done this, you will begin to get a fairly accurate and specific photograph of certain things that you want in your life and around you *daily*. You will also get an awareness of the *quality* of life you are struggling to experience.

Some years ago, I asked a consultant to come into my offices for several days. He was to discuss any complaints or ideas with each of my staff. Then I wanted him to compile a report, unbiased and unprejudiced, as to what he thought about our ministry organization. He interrogated me and questioned me for hours. He would take long walks with me and ride in the car; even while I was in crusades, we would talk on the phone. His constant questioning sharpened my focus remarkably. I have never forgotten it.

He was relentless in collecting data about my personal needs, desires and appetites towards life. When were the *happiest* moments of my life? What days did I seem to enjoy life *more* than usual? What were the 3 biggest problems I thought about *the most* every day? Who were the people that were stressful for me to be around? Who were the people in whose presence I was the most relaxed? How did I want to be remembered? What did I consider to be the most important task that I did each day? Weekly? Monthly? If I had to eliminate 50 percent of my entire ministry workload, what would I *delete?* If I were to have a sudden health crisis, experience a heart attack or some other medical emergency, what would I change *first* about my *daily lifestyle?*

Riveting questions were hurled at me continually. Slowly but surely, a remarkable understanding of what I *really* wanted out of life developed.

Here is a marvelous little exercise. It could change your life forever. Ask one or two of your closest friends, who are skilled at analyzing and dissecting situations, to interrogate you—quizzing you relentlessly, extracting information from you until you have a perfect and complete photograph of the invisible future *you are laboring to bring to reality.* Something is driving you, pushing you toward your future. *What is the invisible dream you are subconsciously trying to birth within you and your life?*

Decisiveness is magnetic.

It is the catalyst for the aura that surrounds extraordinary and unforgettable people. They simply know exactly what they want.

When you are sitting in a restaurant sometime, do a little test. Carefully observe the entry of customers. Notice those who saunter and amble in as if they are not quite certain they have chosen the right restaurant. They slowly walk to their seats wondering if they should even stay at the restaurant, or should they select a different table? Then, observe carefully those who stride in confidently and with a firm, clear and raised voice, express to the hostess of the restaurant, "Good evening! We need a table for 4—by the window, if possible!" Notice how the hostess responds quickly, with enthusiasm and immediately begins to communicate to the other workers exactly what was requested.

When ordering your own meal at a restaurant,

speak up. Speak firmly. Do not mumble.

Someone has said, "If you will raise your voice 10 percent and walk 20 percent faster, you will generate remarkable new energy, compelling others to respond favorably to you and raising the level of self-confidence in every single person around you."

James 1:6-8 says, "But let him ask in faith, nothing wavering. For he that wavereth is like a wave of the sea driven with the wind and tossed. For let not that man think that he shall receive anything of the Lord. A double minded man is unstable in all his ways."

What happens when you are totally undecided about an issue or decision? There is a reason for it. It may be lack of *sufficient* information. It may be lack of accurate information. When this happens, simply declare with great decisiveness, "I have decided to wait 90 days until additional information arrives." You have retained the climate of confidence and decisiveness. Make decisions clearly.

Notice Ruth said it quite clearly, "Whither thou goest, I will go; and where thou lodgest, I will lodge," (Ruth 1:16).

She knew what she wanted. She *communicated* to Naomi what she wanted. She was bold about *what she wanted.*

Distinguish Between What Matters And What Doesn't.

This is one of the Secrets of Champions.

Your Assignment
    Is The Only Place
Your Provision
    Is Guaranteed.

-MIKE MURDOCK

❧ 22 ❧

DISCERN WHERE YOU HAVE BEEN ASSIGNED

━━━━━◗►-◦-◀◖━━━━━

Everything God Has Created Is To Solve A Problem. That is the purpose of creation. Every inventor knows this.

Creativity is merely the solution to current problems.

Mechanics solve automobile problems.

Accountants solve tax problems.

Lawyers solve legal problems.

Mothers solve emotional problems.

Ministers solve spiritual problems.

You were created to solve some kind of problem while you are on earth.

Your Assignment is always to a specific person or to a group of people. Moses' Assignment was to the Israelites. Aaron's Assignment was to Moses.

Your Assignment is always to enable someone to succeed in some area of their life.

Ruth knew her Assignment was specifically to Naomi. She uncluttered her life of any options. Alternatives were not considered. She severed commitments to every other human on earth. She abandoned herself totally to the survival and success of her widowed mother-in-law.

Focus is very powerful. It is magnetic. It is the mysterious secret behind the invisible current called power.

You will only succeed with something that consumes you.

It is the reason many homes have crumbled. The focus has been broken. Many wives are more excited over their boss and job than their husband and children. Many husbands have forgotten to be the priest of their home and protector of their wives. Consumed with their pursuit of financial success or fame in the business world, they have forgotten to whom they have been assigned.

Someone is supposed to succeed because of you. Who is it?

Someone will fail unless your attention is wholly upon them. Who is it?

It astounds me that thousands have no real concern about their place of employment—it is merely a paycheck. It seems their paycheck is of greater priority than the person for whose success they are responsible.

It is a forever memory in my mind. I had finished preaching one night at a great conference here in Dallas, Texas. A very sharp looking young lady had been sitting on the front seat the entire service. She approached me after the service. Her eyes were on fire. Excitement was written all over her countenance.

"I am going to work for you. Somehow... someday...soon. I know I am assigned to you. God told me that tonight." She was very energized as she spoke.

I smiled and said rather quietly, "That is wonderful. I am sure God will direct your steps."

A few weeks later, I walked into my office after flying in from a great crusade. There she was in my office. She had been hired by my office manager as his personal secretary. She seemed vivacious, alive and very enthusiastic. A few weeks later she approached me, and said, "I still feel I am *assigned to you.* Whenever your secretary leaves, I want to apply for that position."

Some weeks later it happened, and I hired her. Within 60 days, she had a fresh and *different* revelation. The pressure was too great. The stress was too continual. When I arrived home from a crusade, she had resigned suddenly, and I did not see her again for a long time. Obviously, she was not really persuaded about her Assignment.

Your Assignment may not appear too appealing initially. I am certain that assisting an elderly widow who was impoverished and broken was not exactly an exciting adventure. But Ruth knew to whom she had been assigned. *Nothing else mattered.*

God created Moses to be a deliverer...to enable the Israelites to move out of captivity.

He created Aaron to hold up the hands of Moses.

He created David to break the tyranny of Saul who was leading Israel into a backslidden state.

He created Jonathan to honor and strengthen David in preparation for kingship.

He created Joseph to make Pharaoh successful and to enable his own family to survive a terrible famine.

Whose success really matters to you?

Whose *failure* would cause you to ache and agonize inside?

Whose pain do you feel?

You may be called to pour healing oil on the broken heart of a battered wife. Injustice may infuriate you, or maybe God has called you to open a home for abused children.

Whatever it is—give yourself totally to your Assignment. It is *only* when you are consumed with another person's success that your own success will emerge.

Is your elderly mother's home neglected and unkept? Do you live a mere hour away? Go to her home. Invest a day of your energy and time. Encourage her, and ease her burden.

Find Your Assignment.

You see, when you are assigned to someone, everything that happens to them *matters to you.* Everything that hurts them...hurts *you.* Everything that brings them joy...brings you *joy.*

Ruth knew when her Assignment had changed.

Few do. Many husbands cannot get away from their mother's apron strings and continue to show divided loyalties. Many wives keep telephoning home and want to go back home for "a while." "Therefore shall a man leave his father and his mother, and shall cleave unto his wife: and they shall be one flesh," (Genesis 2:24).

Your Assignment can change. For a long season of her life, Naomi was Ruth's Assignment. But when Boaz entered her life, the season changed. She did not forsake Naomi, but her devotion to Naomi was a model and monument in the mind of Boaz of what her loyalty to him would be like.

Discern when your Assignment has changed.

Discern Where You Have Been Assigned.

This is one of the Secrets of Champions.

❧ 23 ❧

FOCUS YOUR ENERGY ON YOUR FUTURE

━━━━━━━▷▶◦◀◁━━━━━━━

Become A "Tomorrow Thinker."
Ruth created a future far different from her past.
Ruth was a Moabitess girl raised in heathenism.
Moab was the son of incest between Lot and his daughter. She married Boaz, who one writer said had come through the loins of a temple prostitute by the name of Rahab. God put them together...and ushered in the lineage of Jesus Christ.

Ruth and Boaz produced Obed. Obed produced Jesse. Jesse produced David. David ushered in the lineage of Jesus Christ. Who was Ruth?

Ruth was the great-grandmother of David, the greatest warrior Israel has ever known. She was the great-great-grandmother of one of the wisest men who ever lived on earth, Solomon. Through her and Boaz came the precious Son of the living God, Jesus of Nazareth.

God Never Consults Your Past To Decide Your Future. Satan may remind you of yesterday's mistakes. Do not listen to him. God never reads your diary. Your past is over. Act like it. Talk like it. Live like it.

Your best days are *ahead of you.*
Your worst days are *behind you.*

There Are 3 Kinds of People You Permit In Your Life

Yesterday, Today And Tomorrow People.

Those that God used yesterday may not have a single place in your future.

Do not worry about it. Move quickly toward the promises of God. Prepare to enter your future without yesterday people.

You will not make the mistakes of yesterday again. *You have more knowledge today than you have ever had in your whole lifetime.* You have learned from the *pain.* You have learned from your *losses.* You have watched carefully and documented what's happened in other people's lives.

Do not fear that yesterday will crawl behind you like a predator and choke you to death.

It will not happen. "Remember ye not the former things, neither consider the things of old. Behold, I will do a new thing; now it shall spring forth; shall ye not know it? I will even make a way in the wilderness, and rivers in the desert," (Isaiah 43:18-19).

"Forgetting those things which are behind, and reaching forth unto those things which are before, I press toward the mark," (Philippians 3:13-14).

The Holy Spirit is your Enabler. "But ye shall receive power, after that the Holy Ghost is come upon you," (Acts 1:8).

The Holy Spirit is your Comforter. "But when the Comforter is come, Whom I will send unto you from the Father, even the Spirit of truth," (John 15:26).

The Holy Spirit is your Teacher. "He shall teach you all things, and bring all things to your remembrance, whatsoever I have said unto you," (John 14:26).

The Holy Spirit is the Revealer of those things which are to come. "Howbeit when He, the Spirit of truth, is come, He will guide you into all truth," (John 16:13).

It fascinates me that Ruth was willing to leave everything comfortable to *pursue her future.* Her kinfolks were in her past. She refused to let her upbringing and her religious background become the noose around her neck that sabotaged her future. She refused to let her past rob her of the potential of tomorrow.

I have said many times that *intolerance of the present creates a future.* As long as you can adapt to the present...you really do not have a future.

Ruth refused to build her future around her past. Some of us remember painful experiences from yesterday. We have built our entire lifestyle around that experience. Our conversations are consumed with occurrences of 10 years ago.

This is dangerous.

It is devastating.

When You Discuss Your Past, You Perpetuate It.

Words impart life. When you continually replay painful confrontations and situations of the past, you are giving life to them, you are giving a future to them.

Champions permit yesterday to die.

Ruth did. She did not try to straddle the fence. She refused to become the link between the past and her future.

She totally abandoned the empty relationships of

her past.

One of the saddest pictures is in the life of the great patriarch, Abraham. He insisted on bringing Lot, his nephew, with him into the future God had prepared. Lot was a distraction. Most of Abraham's continual problems could be traced to the *presence of Lot.* You see, God had told him to leave his kinfolks and move on to a different territory. *He insisted on bringing someone he was comfortable with—to the detriment of his future.*

Yesterday people will rarely enjoy your future.

It is natural and normal to want to bring everyone close to us into the chapters of our future success. Few will qualify.

Your future must be *earned.*

It is not guaranteed. It is *not* the same for everyone. Your future is a Harvest produced by the Seeds you are willing to sow. Bringing yesterday people into the future is like using old wineskins for the new wine of tomorrow. It simply will not work.

So, prepare to enter your future without yesterday people. God will bring the right associations with you ...or He has scheduled outstanding Divine connections beyond your greatest and wildest dreams.

Move away from yesterday. You exhausted its benefits. Refuse to waste your energy on repairing it. Rather, rebuild by focusing on your future. Certainly, yesterday can be a reservoir of Wisdom and information. You are not forfeiting loyalty. You are not forgetting the precious lives whom God used mightily for your continual survival and success. But you are refusing to abort your future joys and victories by replaying the memories of yesterday's painful experiences.

Paul refused to wallow in the tears of his past. Few made greater mistakes than he. He caused people to be cast into prison. Christians were murdered because of him. He held the coats of those who stoned the great deacon, Stephen. Yet, he refused to forfeit his future by focusing on his past.

His mistakes were *over.*

His sins were *behind* him.

His name had been *changed.*

Eventually, you will be forced to make a major decision in your life. *It will be the decision to totally abandon your memories, and empty your energy into the palace of your future.*

Your conversation must become more creative. Start using your imagination instead of your memories. Meet new friends. Experience new places.

Ruth knew when she had exhausted the benefits of her present season. This is so powerful and important. Every season in your life contains certain advantages. Whether it is one month of a relationship or 90 days on a job, you must discern the Divine purposes of God in *every situation* in your life. You must discern the Divine purpose of God in *every relationship.*

Never linger in a conversation with someone when it is over. Would you keep chewing the same mouthful of food for 3 hours? Of course not.

Would you keep reading the same page of a book for 3 days? Of course not. Would you leave a broken record on at the same groove replaying the same note over and over again for several hours? Of course not. Would you keep brushing your teeth for 12 hours in a row? Of course not.

When something is finished, it is finished.

Discern it. Recognize it. Look for it. Consistently be intuitive and discerning when a specific season in your life has *concluded.* Then, move *quickly* and *expectantly* to the next season God has arranged for you.

This quality made Ruth unforgettable.

This quality makes champions unforgettable.

Focus Your Energy On Your Future.

This is one of the Secrets of Champions.

RECOMMENDED INVESTMENTS:
The Law of Recognition (Book/B-114/247 pages/$15)
7 Power Keys To Getting What You Want (Book/B-127/32 pages/$7)
Seeds of Wisdom on Productivity (Book/B-137/32 pages/$5)

≈ 24 ≈

EXPECT A NEW GOLDEN CONNECTION EVERY DAY

Successful People Are Observant People.
They notice their *surroundings.*
They notice human *reactions.*
Someone Is Always Observing You Who Is Capable of Greatly Blessing You.
An employer notes laziness instantly. Any boss can tell you who the slow movers are on his staff as well as those who move quickly. It does not necessarily mean that they react instantly to it. Lazy people are not always promoted.

Patterns are studied.

Attitudes are noted.

Promotions are *eventual.*

Boaz, the wealthy landowner, discusses Ruth with his workers one day.

"Who's damsel is this?"

"It is the Moabitish damsel that came back with Naomi out of the country of Moab: And she said, I pray you, let me glean and gather after the reapers among the sheaves: so she came, and hath continued even from the morning until now, that she tarried a little in the house," (Ruth 2:6-7).

Employees notice the most diligent among themselves also. Employees talk to bosses, too. *Bosses listen to trusted employees.* It is quite often that the words of the most trusted employees determine the promotion and salary raises that bosses give throughout the company. That is why it is so foolish to be lazy on your job. Those around you have to carry your part of the workload. They eventually resent you for it. *Their resentment is often spoken into the ears of the only one who can promote you.*

Attitudes become known in the same manner. When one employee is disgruntled or embittered, it permeates and poisons the atmosphere. Eventually, a trusted employee will report it to the supervisor. His removal then is guaranteed. "Know ye not that a little leaven leaveneth the whole lump?" (1 Corinthians 5:6).

"Be not deceived: evil communications corrupt good manners," (1 Corinthians 15:33).

"Where no wood is, there the fire goeth out: so where there is no talebearer, the strife ceaseth," (Proverbs 26:20).

Never forget this. *Your attitude, conduct and behavior is continually being reported to somebody... somewhere...sometime.*

"Therefore whatsoever ye have spoken in darkness shall be heard in the light; and that which ye have spoken in the ear in closets shall be proclaimed upon the housetops," (Luke 12:3). Obviously, critics observe you. They gossip. Ignore the great temptation to become responsive to critics. Suddenly, their opinion can become your focus. You will strive to justify your behavior or become entangled in an internal campaign to prove them wrong.

Do not fall for it.

Critics rarely present a plan for improvement.
They are not builders. They are destroyers.

Never build your life around the opinion of a critic.

Rather, become conscious that whoever God has ordained to be your golden connection to the next season of your life—*is presently observing you.*

They study your reactions in a crisis.

They note your response to criticism and correction.

They listen for an attitude of humility, kindness and graciousness.

Your acts of mercy are documented.

Every Good Quality In You Is Obvious And Noticeable To The One God Has Called To Promote You.

Ruth did not have to "sell" herself to Boaz. She did not have to speak persuasively and coyly nor be flirtatious with his servants.

In fact, let me reassure you that had she been flirting with the workers, Boaz would have been the first person to know it. News travels. People discuss each other.

And consequently, Ruth would never have become Mrs. Boaz.

Great People Notice Great Qualities.

So do not become discouraged when criticism hits you from every side.

Do not become frustrated when it seems that promotion is coming slowly, and you wonder if God really has noticed your hard efforts and consistency to please Him.

There is a Boaz scheduled in your future.

He may already be in your present season.

There is a strong possibility that he already knows you by name and is making plans to bless you and cause great experiences in your life.

Somebody is saying some good things about you today.

Somebody sees the rare qualities within you.

Something incredible is being spoken about your life.

Somebody is planning to reward you.

They are closer than you even realize.

Your faith will decide when it happens.

Your *attitude* schedules it.

So keep your focus on *obedience.*

Keep your focus on doing the right things.

When you keep doing the right things, the right people will enter your life.

When you keep doing the right things, *the wrong people will disconnect from you.*

When you keep doing the right things, news gets around.

When you keep doing the rights things, *promotion is guaranteed.*

"Then said Boaz unto Ruth, Hearest thou not, my daughter? Go not to glean in another field, neither go from hence, but abide here fast by my maidens: Let thine eyes be on the field that they do reap, and go thou after them: have I not charged the young men that they shall not touch thee? and when thou art athirst, go unto the vessels, and drink of that which the young men have drawn," (Ruth 2:8-9). Boaz told his young men to let her glean right among the sheaves without stopping her, and to snap off some heads of barley and drop them on purpose for her to glean, and not make any remarks (see verses 15 and 16).

Never forget this.

Your father is noting your response to his correction. Your mother senses your desire to show mercy to your sisters and brothers.

Your brothers and sisters eventually get a report on your true attitude and feelings about them.

Your boss discovers quicker than you could possibly realize when you disagree with an instruction he has given you.

Somebody is observing you today who is in a position to launch the greatest season of miracles you have ever known in your entire lifetime.

Do not take it lightly. Guard your words. Guard your attitude.

"A good name is rather to be chosen than great riches," (Proverbs 22:1).

It will make you *unforgettable.*

Expect A New Golden Connection Every Day.

This is one of the Secrets of Champions.

RECOMMENDED INVESTMENTS:
Seeds of Wisdom on Relationships (Book/B-14/32 pages/$3)
Seeds of Wisdom on Miracles (Book/B-15/32 pages/$3)
The Law of Recognition (Book/B-114/247 pages/$15)

When God Wants
To Bless You,
He Brings A Person
Into Your Life.

-MIKE MURDOCK

≈ 25 ≈

EXUDE GRATITUDE CONTINUOUSLY

Champions Are Thankful And Appreciative.
Ruth was *appreciative*.

Appreciative means, "showing appreciation of someone or something; to be grateful."

It is interesting to note the reaction of Ruth when Boaz gave her permission to stay in his field and glean barley. She thanked him warmly. "Then she fell on her face, and bowed herself to the ground, and said unto him, Why have I found grace in thine eyes, that they shouldest take knowledge of me, seeing I am a stranger? And Boaz answered and said unto her, It hath fully been shewed me, all that thou hast done unto thy mother in law since the death of thine husband," (Ruth 2:10-11).

She continues on in verse 13, "Then she said, Let me find favour in thy sight, my lord; for that thou hast comforted me, and for that thou hast spoken friendly unto thine handmaid, though I be not like unto one of thine handmaidens." She did not *assume* that it was *owed* her. She really did not even ask for extra favor. She valued the smallest crumb or barley left in her behalf.

Appreciative people have a magnetism to them. Their ability to value acts of kindness inspire us and make us want to perform accordingly.

Jessica is a beautiful little 9 year old girl in

Minneapolis, Minnesota. She is so articulate, expressive and appreciative. Every time I have done something special for her, she looks up with those big beautiful eyes and the biggest smile you can imagine, and says, "Oh, thank you so very much!" It is the attitude of appreciation that makes children so delightful and makes us want to produce for them.

It is often said that Christmas is for children. Now why do we say this when it is celebrated as the birthday of Jesus of Nazareth? Why doesn't every one of us enjoy Christmas like children?

Children *appreciate.*

They celebrate gifts.

Gifts are great events to them.

It is so unfortunate that after some of us receive so many gifts and blessings for so many years, our ability to appreciate seems to deteriorate and diminish dramatically. Work on this in your personal life. Work on this in your home. Do not take for granted that your husband is "supposed to bring home the paycheck." Do not assume that it is "a woman's place to clean up the house and prepare the meals."

Appreciation of those around you will make you unforgettable.

Find ways to express your appreciation.

Do it *verbally.* Speak kind words of appreciation.

Do it *privately.* When no one else is around, be gentle in expressing your true appreciation and gratefulness.

Do it *publicly.* Others need to hear that you know and appreciate what God has blessed you with.

Do it *often.* Not just once a year at a birthday or

an anniversary.

Do it *generously.* Go the extra mile when you buy a gift for someone special whom you love and appreciate.

Do it *thoughtfully.* One of my closest friends in Sarasota, Florida, sent me two books a few weeks ago. What kind of books? The very author that he knows I love to read. He had put *thought* into the purchase of my gifts. He knew what I wanted to read. I have had many people give me books *they* thought I *ought* to read...very few have purchased me books that I *wanted* to read.

Do it *quickly.* If someone has blessed your life significantly, do not wait several months or years to express it. Try to establish the habit of responding to an act of kindness *within 72 hours.*

Do it *cheerfully.* When you express your appreciation, do not do it grudgingly as if it is a pain or an effort.

You will become *unforgettable* to every friend in your life.

Exude Gratitude Continuously.
This is one of the Secrets of Champions.

Every Environment Requires
A Code of Conduct
For Entering Or
Remaining In It.

-MIKE MURDOCK

⚍ 26 ⚎

EMBRACE THE PROTOCOL
AND LAW OF THE HOUSE

═══════►▷-◉-◁◄═══════

Authority Creates Order.

It was the custom for a widow to marry the nearest kinsman, who could purchase the ground of her dead husband, and then perpetuate the Seed through children. Naomi gave Ruth that privilege by encouraging her to approach Boaz. And Ruth replied to Naomi, "All that thou sayest unto me I will do. And she went down unto the floor, and did according to all that her mother in law bade her," (Ruth 3:5-6).

Tradition contains limitations.

Custom is not *always* in the best interest of locality.

Established protocol can be questioned.

However, there is a great benefit in respecting authority. *Great favor flows when the rules of conduct are appreciated and respected.*

Most of us learn from books on etiquette, or caring mothers and friends who reprove us when we get out of hand.

Acceptable rules of behavior are valuable. They bond people. They link people. They create the comfortable climate that launches friendships.

Relationships Are Strengthened Because of Protocol.

Ruth was from Moab. She was unfamiliar with the customs of Naomi's people. But she knew the incredible *rewards of cooperation.* Remember this.

Champions Know The Rewards of Cooperation.

Those who do not treasure the rewards of cooperation often wind up in prison or unemployed.

The purpose of authority is to create order.

Order Is The Accurate Arrangement of Things.

The purpose of order is to increase your productivity.

Productivity determines your rewards.

This explains red lights and stop signs. It explains speed limits. Rules increase safety and the protection of us all.

Attend seminars, read books and listen to tapes that show you the rules of conduct and guidelines for social behavior with others.

3 Rewards of Honoring Protocol

1. It Will Multiply Your Effectiveness In Communication.

2. It Will Increase Your Ability To Make Friends.

3. It Can Reduce The Number of Enemies Throughout Your Lifetime.

Embrace The Protocol And Law of The House.

It is a Master Secret in the life of Champions.

❦ 27 ❦

BECOME KNOWN FOR INTEGRITY

People Talk.

Everyone knew about Ruth.

Boaz describes it this way, "It hath fully been shewed me, all that thou hast done unto thy mother in law since the death of thine husband: and how thou hast left thy father and thy mother, and the land of thy nativity, and art come unto a people which thou knewest not heretofore," (Ruth 2:11).

Later he spoke, "Blessed be thou of the Lord, my daughter: for thou hast shewed me more kindness in the latter end than at the beginning, inasmuch as thou followedst not young men, whether rich or poor...for all the city of my people know that thou art a virtuous woman," (Ruth 3:10-11).

People talk. Good things and bad things. False accusations and current assessments.

People spoke well of her. Her sacrificial attitude and dedication to preserving and maintaining the life of her widowed mother-in-law was a known fact in the community. Obviously, she had not even dated or bonded with any of the young men in the city—rich or poor. Her total focus was on Naomi.

Productivity is a choice.

This had registered heavily in the heart and mind of Boaz who did not hesitate to respond to her pursuit of him.

Others should commend you. "Let another man praise thee, and not thine own mouth," (Proverbs 27:2).

Reputation is more powerful than money. "A good name is rather to be chosen than great riches," (Proverbs 22:1).

A good name is more magnetic than a strong fragrance. "A good name is better than precious ointment," (Ecclesiastes 7:1).

Several years ago, I arrived at the house of a young lady to take her to supper. As we were driving to the restaurant she remarked: "I had another date planned tonight, but I told him I had to visit a relative in the hospital."

She had lied. It sickened me. I had been excited about establishing a relationship with her only to find out within minutes that falsehood came naturally and easily to her. Obviously, I would be the next victim on her list. It was the first and last date I had with her.

Whatever it takes, develop integrity.

Focus on it. Carefully examine each word and sentence that comes from your lips. Never say anything insincere. Refuse to brag on someone's singing if it is untrue. Do not say things merely to encourage others. "Recompense to no man evil for evil. Provide things honest in the sight of all men," (Romans 12:17).

The *compassion* of Ruth was known.

Observe how a woman speaks to her mother. Note well how a man treats his mother. Also, observe how he reacts to the struggles and heartaches of the unfortunate.

Ruth's purity and virtue were known. Admittedly, many false accusations are hurled these days. Good people have been stained through vindictive and violent people. Joseph is not the only story where someone who has walked totally before the Lord had his reputation devastated by those who had been refused or ignored.

However, the entire town knew of her obsession and kindness to her mother-in-law. *They said she treated her mother-in-law better than seven sons would treat a mother.* That kind of treatment is almost unheard of these days.

This does not mean you have to advertise all your good deeds. It is not important that you trumpet to the world all your acts of kindness and mercy. Somehow, God has a way of "letting it be made known."

What you are will eventually be exposed and known.

Yes, these are marvelous qualities that make you unforgettable.

Become Known For Integrity.

This is one of the Secrets of Champions.

RECOMMENDED INVESTMENTS:
Wisdom For Crisis Times (Book/B-40/112 pages/$9)
Thirty-One Secrets of an Unforgettable Woman (Book/B-57/
    140 pages/$12)
Seven Obstacles To Abundant Success (Book/B-64/32 pages/$5)
The Holy Spirit Handbook (Book/B-100/153 pages/$15)

The Proof of Humility
Is The Willingness
To Change.

-MIKE MURDOCK

❧ 28 ❧

MAKE NECESSARY ADJUSTMENTS CONTINUALLY

Appearance Matters.

Ruth worked in the fields gathering barley or wheat, depending on the season. One day, she came home and was sitting there with Naomi. Her hair was probably matted, sweat pouring down her body. She was exhausted and worn out. Undoubtedly, she looked as bad as anyone could look at the end of a long, hard day.

Naomi gives her advice about approaching Boaz. "Wash thyself therefore, and anoint thee, and put thy raiment upon thee, and get thee down to the floor," (Ruth 3:3).

Men respond to *sight.*

Women respond to *touch.*

I do not know all the details, but all of us will agree that men and women are totally different creatures.

Needs differ.

Tastes differ.

Hygiene matters.

Appearance matters.

Ruth packaged herself for where she was going, instead of where she had been.

The attire of a *harlot* is discussed in Proverbs 7.

The attire of a *virtuous woman* is discussed in Proverbs 31.

In Genesis, Joseph shaved his beard and changed his raiment because the Egyptians hated beards. He wanted to *create a climate of acceptance* in the palace of Pharaoh.

Even Timothy was instructed by the Apostle Paul on the appearance and clothing of women in the church.

I attended an amazing seminar some months ago. It was on appearance and how to create a sense of balance with clothing, even to changing the colors you were wearing.

Packaging Determines Desire.

Naomi was brilliant. She taught Ruth how to give Boaz *a picture he would want to remember.* A picture that gave him a desire to reach.

Some months ago, I was driving by a home. The wife was waving good-bye to her husband as he was backing out of the driveway. Her hair was in curlers. Her bathrobe looked torn, wrinkled and probably had a button or two missing. I was not close enough to smell her breath, but I certainly could imagine it! She was waving to him goodbye and *giving him a permanent photograph of what was awaiting him upon his return home.* (Maybe that explained why he couldn't wait to get to work!)

I had to laugh inside. I could just imagine his thoughts of "home" as he drove by the billboards of beautiful ladies and walked into his office with everyone packaged nicely and attractively.

What am I saying? *You must make yourself desirable for the man you desire.*

The president of the largest employment agency in the world said that over 90 percent of the people who are hired were hired because of their personal appearance.

You are a walking message system. People *see* what you are *before they hear* what you are.

Imagine riding on an airplane and noticing that the pilot has catsup all over his shirt. Imagine his hair uncombed. Imagine dirt all over the bottom of his shoes. Now, try to imagine sitting in the seat and noticing torn seat covers on your seat. Several light bulbs are smashed. What is your next thought? "I wonder if anyone has *checked the engine?* I wonder if there is enough *fuel* in the tanks? I wonder if they have had the mechanics provide accurate maintenance?"

Packaging Determines Whether You Reach Or Withdraw.

Look at the products you purchase at the store.

Everything you are buying is based on... *appearance.*

Make any change necessary today that will make you more desirable to your man. It may be braces on your teeth, taking your clothes to the cleaners for pressing, or finding the lipstick with exactly the right color for you.

This kind of attitude made Ruth an unforgettable woman, and this kind of attitude will make you an unforgettable Champion.

Make Necessary Adjustments Continually.

This is one of the Secrets of Champions.

The Passion of The Protégé
Is Revealed By
The Pursuit of The Mentor.

-MIKE MURDOCK

❧ 29 ❧

BECOME A PROTÉGÉ TO AN UNCOMMON MENTOR

━━━━━◦❖◦━━━━━

A Mentor Is A Trusted Teacher.

Your Mentor sees your future before you do.

Mentors are not necessarily cheerleaders. A Mentor is a coach. Their role is not merely to confirm what you are doing correctly. Their goal is to *correct* you and prevent you from making a mistake.

There are 2 ways to learn:

1.   Mistakes, or

2.   Mentors.

In Scriptures, Ruth is a remarkable example of a Protégé.

Ruth had not remarried when she followed Naomi back to Bethlehem.

She worked hard. One day, Naomi expressed that it was time for her to have a husband in her life. She advised her to go to the threshing floor where Boaz worked every night. Naomi knew the habits of extraordinary men.

Great Men Simply Have Great Habits.

She advised Ruth to avoid discussions with him while he was having supper or even working. She instructed Ruth that there would be an *appropriate time* that Boaz would awaken, see her and discuss any details regarding a relationship.

Ruth *listened*. She followed the instructions. And history records the incredible parade of benefits that followed.

Ruth was *teachable*. Boaz had instructed her to restrict her work and the gathering of food to his fields alone and not go into other fields. Naomi had given the same instructions. Ruth followed them.

Hearing good advice is *not* the key to success.

Applying good advice is the key to extraordinary success.

One of my pastor friends has had remarkable success in his ministry. He shared with me one day an important key concerning counseling.

"Mike, I refuse to counsel anyone personally until they have sat in every single service in which I have ministered for a period of 6 weeks. If their questions and problems have not been resolved through my teaching over a 6 week period, I will schedule a personal counseling session with them. In that session, I give specific instructions to be followed. If they do not follow those instructions, I refuse to give a second counseling session. It is a waste of my time and theirs, if they refuse to implement the Wisdom I impart."

You can predict the success of someone by their ability to follow instructions.

I am praying that God returns a real respect for the elderly of our generation. Some older women in our generation have more insight and Wisdom in their little finger than many young girls will have within the next 20 years of their lives.

Elisha sat at the feet of Elijah.

Timothy sat at the feet of Paul.

Esther listened to Mordecai and the eunuch who advised her.

Joshua sat at the feet of Moses.

Your Mentor foresees problems you cannot see coming.

Are you planning to enter the field of real estate? Find the most successful and productive realtor within 100 miles. Establish a friendship. Become the Protégé.

Do you long for a useful ministry? Find a man or woman of God to serve. Carry their briefcase. Shine their shoes. Babysit their children. Clean their house. Wash their car. *Do whatever is necessary to access their anointing, connect with their climate and attach yourself to their atmosphere.*

Whatever is growing in them will begin to grow within you.

Whatever they have decided to starve will die within you.

Ruth applied good advice when she heard it. It made her *unforgettable.*

5 Facts About Mentorship

1. You Will Usually Have More Than One Mentor In Your Life. Financial, spiritual and academic Mentors exist everywhere.

2. Different Kinds of Mentorships Exist. Some of us are mentored through tapes, books and relationships. However, there can always be a primary Mentor who remains with you throughout your life.

My father is the most important Mentor in my daily life. For many years I struggled to impress him rather than receive from him. I wanted him to celebrate my discoveries rather than sit and absorb his own discoveries. After understanding mentorship, now I LEARN MORE FROM HIM IN A SINGLE DAY THAN I USED TO LEARN IN A YEAR. Pursue, cherish and protect your gift from God, your Mentor.

3. Respect And Protect The Access Your Mentor Permits You. He will not always be there. You must face some battles alone. So drink deeply from his well now while you have access.

4. Treasure Any Invitation For Private Discussion With Your Mentor. The presence of others changes the level of intimacy and information. When I am alone with my father, I receive much more than I do when others are present. The information is more specific. Exact. Precise. *Just for me.* The thought and opinions of others present often dilute and even weaken the impartation.

5. Your Mentor Often Discerns Whether You Discern His Worth Or Not. No words need to be spoken. Flattering words are unnecessary. Persuasive words do not matter. When you are in the presence of someone who truly respects what you know, you detect it instantly.

Become A Protégé To An Uncommon Mentor.

This is one of the Secrets of Champions.

RECOMMENDED INVESTMENTS:
The Gift of Wisdom For Achievers (Book/B-68/32 pages/$10)
31 Secrets of The Uncommon Mentor (6 tapes/TS-37/$30)

❧ 30 ❧

SOW FAVOR GENEROUSLY

Favor Is Your Seed Into Others.

Favor Is The Divine Current That Takes You From Your Present Season Into Your Future Dream.

Favor Is The Golden Link From Your Pit To Your Palace.

10 Facts About Favor

1.   Favor Is When Someone Has A Desire To Solve A Problem For You. Your own attitude determines God's attitude toward you. Follow the path of favor *wherever it is happening* in your life today. Who has discerned your worth? Who feels *kindly* toward your life? Who has been *the source most used* by God in your financial life within the last 12 months?   Who has been your greatest source of spiritual *encouragement* and maturity? Who does God seem to be using *right now to open appropriate doors* for your life? Who is the Golden Connection that could easily shorten the trip that you have been taking toward your dream?

Recognize the *path.*

Recognize the *person.*

God is presently using them for this *season.* (Stop evaluating their flaws. Stop building walls of distrust. Is God using them in your own life *right now?*)

2.   Favor Is A Gift From God. He does not

owe it to you. You cannot purchase it. Others are not obligated to you. (When you obligate others, you create a potential enemy. Those acts are called favors, not favor.) "He that openeth, and no man shutteth," (Revelation 3:7).

3. Favor Is Necessary For Uncommon Success. You cannot work hard enough to get everything you deserve and want. You cannot work enough jobs to generate the finances you will need for all your dreams and goals. Others owe you nothing. Yet favor is necessary for you to take giant leaps into your future. "The Lord thy God shall bless thee in all thine increase, and in all the works of thine hands," (Deuteronomy 16:15).

4. Favor Begins When You Solve A Problem For Someone. When Joseph interpreted the dream for Pharaoh, his gift made room for him. He was promoted to the second place of power, Prime Minister. "And Pharaoh took off his ring from his hand, and put it upon Joseph's hand, and arrayed him in vestures of fine linen, and put a gold chain about his neck; And he made him to ride in the second chariot which he had; and they cried before him, Bow the knee: and he made him ruler over all the land of Egypt. And Pharaoh said unto Joseph, I am Pharaoh, and without thee shall no man lift up his hand or foot in all the land of Egypt," (Genesis 41:42-44).

5. Favor Is A Seed You Can Sow Into Others. *Everyone has the ability to sow favor.* Solving problems are Seeds of favor. Enabling others to succeed reveals favor. When you help others achieve their goals, you are sowing favor. "Knowing that whatsoever good thing any man doeth, the same shall he receive of the Lord, whether he be bond or free," (Ephesians 6:8).

Favor Begins As A Seed And Ends As A Harvest. What you sow today will re-enter your life in your future. This is the Harvest of Favor. "Be not deceived; God is not mocked: for whatsoever a man soweth, that shall he also reap," (Galatians 6:7).

6. **Favor Can Stop When You Deliberately Ignore An Instruction From God.** Saul ignored the instructions of Samuel to kill King Agag, and all the Amalekites. Favor stopped. God altered the monarchy and David became king. "But Saul and the people spared Agag...Then came the word of the Lord unto Samuel, saying, It repenteth Me that I have set up Saul to be king...for thou hast rejected the word of the Lord, and the Lord hath rejected thee from being king over Israel," (1 Samuel 15:9-11, 26).

Nebuchadnezzar experienced uncommon success. When he became filled with pride, God let him become like a beast in the field for seven years. "But when his heart was lifted up, and his mind hardened in pride, he was deposed from his kingly throne, and they took his glory from him...and his heart was made like the beasts," (Daniel 5:20-21).

7. **Favor Stops When The Tithe Is Withheld From God.** A curse comes instead of a blessing. "Will a man rob God? Yet ye have robbed Me. But ye say, Wherein have we robbed Thee? In tithes and offerings. Ye are cursed with a curse: for ye have robbed Me, even this whole nation," (Malachi 3:8-9).

8. **Favor Can Make You Wealthy In One Day.** The peasant Ruth became the wife of the wealthy Boaz. "So Boaz took Ruth, and she was his wife," (Ruth 4:13).

9. Favor Can Stop A Tragedy Instantly. Favor prevents tragedies. It moved Joseph from the prison to the palace in 24 hours. "And Pharaoh said unto Joseph...Thou shalt be over my house, and according unto thy word shall all my people be ruled," (Genesis 41:39-40). When Jonah cried out on the streets of Ninevah, favor flowed. God had sent Jonah to warn the Ninevites. When the king called a fast, the favor of God was birthed. (See Jonah 3:10.)

10. Favor Can Grow. Jesus grew in favor with God and man. (See Luke 2:52.) The good happening for you today can increase 100 times within the next 12 months. "Then Peter began to say unto Him, Lo, we have left all, and have followed Thee. And Jesus answered and said, Verily I say unto you, There is no man that hath left house, or brethren, or sisters, or father, or mother, or wife, or children, or lands, for My sake, and the gospel's, But he shall receive an hundredfold now in this time, houses, and brethren, and sisters, and mothers, and children, and lands, with persecutions; and in the world to come eternal life," (Mark 10:28-30).

Sow Favor Generously.

This is one of the Secrets of Champions.

RECOMMENDED INVESTMENTS:
Seeds of Wisdom on Seed-Faith (Book/B-16/32 pages/$3)
Secrets of the Richest Man Who Ever Lived (Book/B-99/
    179 pages/$12)

～ 31 ～

NEVER DO WHAT A MACHINE CAN DO

Proper Equipment Increases Your Productivity.
Never have someone do a job that a machine can do instead. This is a humorous explanation of the advantages of proper machines.

10 Advantages In Using Appropriate Technology

1.   Machines Do Not *Require Coaxing,* Just Repair.

2.   Machines Do Not Get *Discouraged* When Their Mother-in-law Comes To Town.

3.   Machines Are Never *Disloyal,* Discussing Your Secrets With Everyone Else.

4.   Your Machines Will Not *File Grievance Reports* Against You When You Fail To Meet Their Expectations.

5.   Machines Do Not Require *Medical Insurance,* Sick Leave Or Time Off.

6.   Machines Can Be *Replaced* Quickly And Easily Without Breaking Your Heart.

7.   Machines Do Not *Request A Retirement Fund* And Want To Be Paid For The Years Ahead When They Do Not Perform.

8.   Machines Never Come To Work *Late*

And Want To *Leave Early.*

9.   Machines Will Work *Through* Lunch, Requiring No "Break Time."

10.   Machines Never Interrupt The Productivity of *Other Machines,* Slowing Down The Entire Project.

6 Qualities of True Achievers...They Will:

1.   Find The Most Effective Equipment Possible To Do Their Present Job.

2.   Telephone Other Businesses Or Companies To Locate Appropriate Or Needed Machines And Equipment.

3.   Attend Seminars And Workshops That Increase Their Efficiency Or Skills On Computers And Other Machines.

4.   Inform Their Boss What Is Needed To Do The Job More Efficiently, More Accurately And Quickly. (He will usually do anything possible to make the hours of employees more effective and productive.)

5.   Continuously Evaluate Their Work. What is slowing them down? What machine could make a big difference in the completion of their daily tasks and responsibilities?

6.   Present Their Supervisors With Options, Costs And Potential Benefits of Purchasing More Machines. Your Staff will treasure it and learn to appreciate their own work load reduction because of it. It decreases the opportunities for mistakes. It increases their sense of progress and accomplishment. Search for appropriate equipment to accomplish your tasks quickly.

Never Do What A Machine Can Do.

This is one of the Secrets of Champions.

DECISION

Will You Accept Jesus As Your Personal Savior Today?

The Bible says, "That if thou shalt confess with thy mouth the Lord Jesus, and shalt believe in thine heart that God hath raised Him from the dead, thou shalt be saved," (Romans 10:9).

Pray this prayer from your heart today!

"Dear Jesus, I believe that You died for me and rose again on the third day. I confess I am a sinner...I need Your love and forgiveness...Come into my heart. Forgive my sins. I receive Your eternal life. Confirm Your love by giving me peace, joy and supernatural love for others. Amen."

DR. MIKE MURDOCK

is in tremendous demand as one of the most dynamic speakers in America today.

More than 16,000 audiences in 40 countries have attended his Schools of Wisdom and conferences. Hundreds of invitations come to him from churches, colleges and business corporations. He is a noted author of over 200 books, including the best sellers, *The Leadership Secrets of Jesus* and *Secrets of the Richest Man Who Ever Lived.* Thousands view his weekly television program, *Wisdom Keys with Mike Murdock.* Many attend his Schools of Wisdom that he hosts in many cities of America.

☐ Yes, Mike! I made a decision to accept Christ as my personal Savior today. Please send me my free gift of your book, *31 Keys to a New Beginning* to help me with my new life in Christ.

NAME _____ BIRTHDAY _____

ADDRESS _____

CITY _____ STATE ____ ZIP _____

PHONE _____ E-MAIL _____

Mail to: **The Wisdom Center** · 4051 Denton Hwy. · Ft. Worth, TX 76117
1-817-759-BOOK · 1-817-759-0300
You Will Love Our Website...! WisdomOnline.com

DR. MIKE MURDOCK

1 Has embraced his Assignment to Pursue...Proclaim...and Publish the Wisdom of God to help people achieve their dreams and goals.

2 Preached his first public sermon at the age of 8.

3 Preached his first evangelistic crusade at the age of 15.

4 Began full-time evangelism at the age of 19, which has continued since 1966.

5 Has traveled and spoken to more than 16,000 audiences in 40 countries, including East and West Africa, the Orient, Europe and South America.

6 Noted author of over 200 books, including best sellers, *Wisdom for Winning, Dream Seeds, The Double Diamond Principle, The Law of Recognition* and *The Holy Spirit Handbook.*

7 Created the popular *Topical Bible* series for Businessmen, Mothers, Fathers, Teenagers; *The One-Minute Pocket Bible* series, and *The Uncommon Life* series.

8 The Creator of the Master 7 Mentorship Program, an Achievement Program for Believers.

9 Has composed thousands of songs such as "I Am Blessed," "You Can Make It," "God Rides On Wings of Love" and "Jesus, Just The Mention of Your Name," recorded by many gospel artists.

10 Is the Founder and Senior Pastor of The Wisdom Center, in Fort Worth, Texas...a Church with International Ministry around the world.

11 Host of *Wisdom Keys with Mike Murdock,* a weekly TV Program seen internationally.

12 Has appeared often on TBN, CBN, BET, Daystar, Inspirational Network, LeSea Broadcasting and other television network programs.

13 Has led over 3,000 to accept the call into full-time ministry.

128

THE MINISTRY

1 **Wisdom Books & Literature** - Over 200 best-selling Wisdom Books and 70 Teaching Tape Series.

2 **Church Crusades** - Multitudes are ministered to in crusades and seminars throughout America in "The Uncommon Wisdom Conferences." Known as a man who loves pastors, he has focused on church crusades for over 41 years.

3 **Music Ministry** - Millions have been blessed by the anointed songwriting and singing of Mike Murdock, who has made over 15 music albums and CDs available.

4 **Television** - *Wisdom Keys with Mike Murdock,* a nationally-syndicated weekly television program.

5 **The Wisdom Center** - The Church and Ministry Offices where Dr. Murdock speaks weekly on Wisdom for The Uncommon Life.

6 **Schools of The Holy Spirit** - Mike Murdock hosts Schools of The Holy Spirit in many churches to mentor believers on the Person and Companionship of The Holy Spirit.

7 **Schools of Wisdom** - In many major cities Mike Murdock hosts Schools of Wisdom for those who want personalized and advanced training for achieving "The Uncommon Dream."

8 **Missions Outreach** - Dr. Mike Murdock's overseas outreaches to 40 countries have included crusades in East and West Africa, the Orient, Europe and South America.

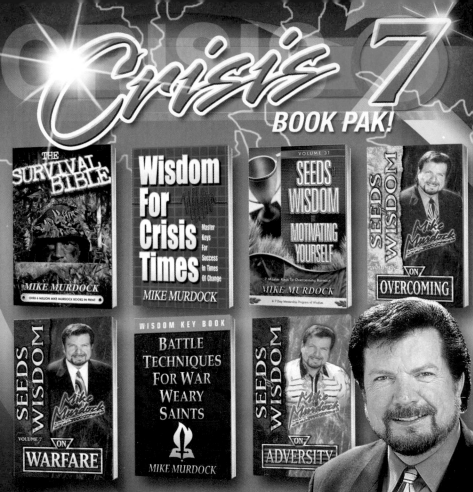

Crisis 7 BOOK PAK!

DR. MIKE MURDOCK

❶ **The Survival Bible** (Book/B-29/248pg/$10)

❷ **Wisdom For Crisis Times** (Book/B-40/112pg/$9)

❸ **Seeds of Wisdom on Motivating Yourself** (Book/B-171/32pg/$5)

❹ **Seeds of Wisdom on Overcoming** (Book/B-17/32pg/$3)

❺ **Seeds of Wisdom on Warfare** (Book/B-19/32pg/$3)

❻ **Battle Techniques For War-Weary Saints** (Book/B-07/32pg/$5)

❼ **Seeds of Wisdom on Adversity** (Book/B-21/32pg/$3)

The Wisdom Center
Crisis 7 Book Pak!
Only $30 $36 Value
WBL-25
Wisdom Is The Principal Thing

Add 20% For S/H

Quantity Prices Available Upon Request

Each Wisdom Book may be purchased separately if so desired.

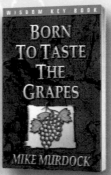

101 Wisdom Keys That Have Most Changed My Life.

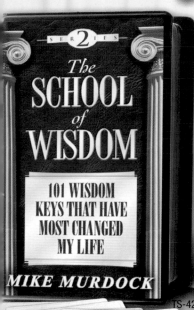

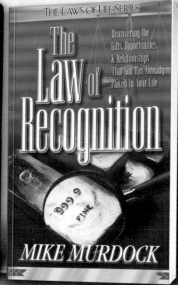

TS-42

School of Wisdom #2 Pak!

- ▶ What Attracts Others Toward You
- ▶ The Secret Of Multiplying Your Financial Blessings
- ▶ What Stops The Flow Of Your Faith
- ▶ Why Some Fail And Others Succeed
- ▶ How To Discern Your Life Assignment
- ▶ How To Create Currents Of Favor With Others
- ▶ How To Defeat Loneliness
- ▶ 47 Keys In Recognizing The Mate God Has Approved For You
- ▶ 14 Facts You Should Know About Your Gifts And Talents
- ▶ 17 Important Facts You Should Remember About Your Weakness
- ▶ And Much, Much More...

The Wisdom Center
School of Wisdom #2 Pak!
Only $**30** $40 Value
PAK002
Wisdom Is The Principal Thing

Add 20% For S/H

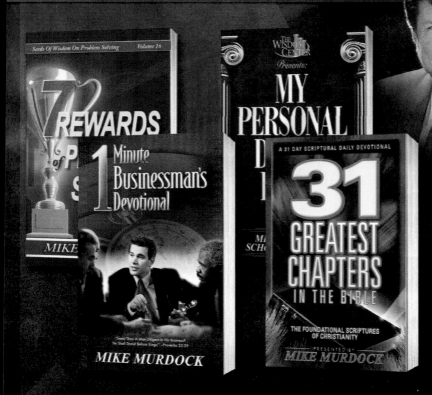

Millionaire-Talk

SCHOOL of FINANCIAL SUCCESS SERIES

31 THINGS You Will Need To Become A MILLIONAIRE

Your Financial Future Is Determined By The Instruction You Are Willing To Follow.

FREE BOOK ENCLOSED!

MASTER 7 MENTORSHIP PROGRAM of Mike Murdock

DR. MIKE MURDOCK

MY GIFT OF APPRECIATION
GIFT of Appreciation
Wisdom Is The Principal Thing

31 Things You Will Need To Become A Millionaire (2-CD's/WCPL-116)

Topics Include:
- You Will Need Financial Heroes
- Your Willingness To Negotiate Everything
- You Must Have The Ability To Transfer Your Enthusiasm, Your Vision To Others
- Know Your Competition
- Be Willing To Train Your Team Personally As To Your Expectations
- Hire Professionals To Do A Professional's Job

I have asked the Lord for 3,000 special partners who will sow an extra Seed of $58 towards our Television Outreach Ministry. Your Seed is so appreciated! Remember to request your Gift CD's, 2 Disc Volume, *31 Things You Will Need To Become A Millionaire*, when you write this week!

THE WISDOM CENTER
4051 Denton Highway • Fort Worth, TX 76117
1-817-759-BOOK
1-817-759-0300

You Will Love Our Website...!
WISDOMONLINE.COM

G

The CRISIS COLLECTION

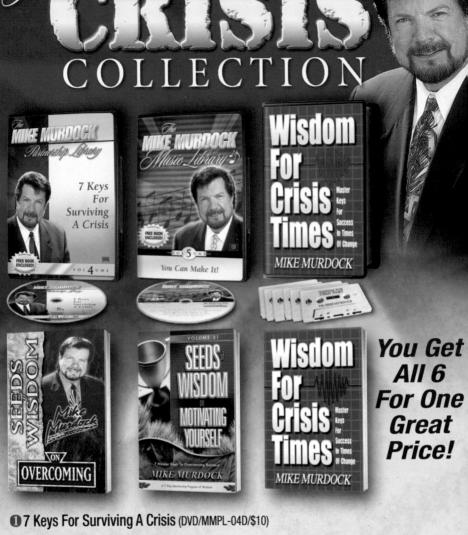

You Get All 6 For One Great Price!

❶ **7 Keys For Surviving A Crisis** (DVD/MMPL-04D/$10)

❷ **You Can Make It!** (Music CD/MMML-05/$10)

❸ **Wisdom For Crisis Times** (6 Cassettes/TS-40/$30)

❹ **Seeds of Wisdom on Overcoming** (Book/B-17/32pg/$3)

❺ **Seeds of Wisdom on Motivating Yourself** (Book/B-171/32pg/$5)

❻ **Wisdom For Crisis Times** (Book/B-40/112pg/$9)

Also Included... Two Free Bonus Books!

Each Wisdom Product may be purchased separately if so desired.

The Wisdom Center

The Crisis Collection

Only $40 $87 Value

PAK-16

Wisdom Is The Principal Thing

Add 20% For S/H

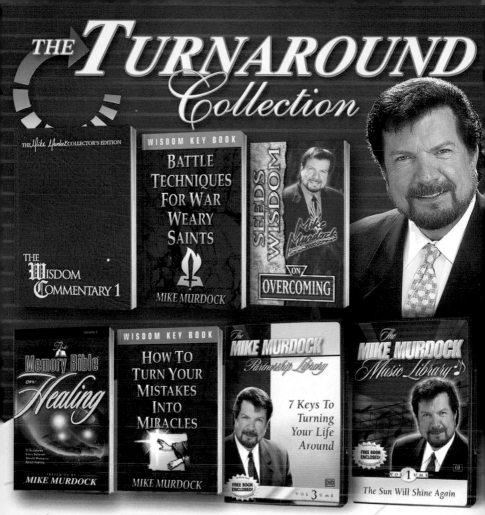

THE TURNAROUND Collection

WISDOM KEY BOOK
BATTLE TECHNIQUES FOR WAR WEARY SAINTS
MIKE MURDOCK

THE Mike Murdock COLLECTOR'S EDITION
THE WISDOM COMMENTARY 1

SEEDS of WISDOM on OVERCOMING

WISDOM KEY BOOK
HOW TO TURN YOUR MISTAKES INTO MIRACLES
MIKE MURDOCK

Volume 2
The Memory Bible on Healing
PRESENTED BY MIKE MURDOCK

The MIKE MURDOCK Partnership Library
7 Keys To Turning Your Life Around
FREE BOOK ENCLOSED!
VOLUME 3

The MIKE MURDOCK Music Library
FREE BOOK ENCLOSED!
VOLUME 1
The Sun Will Shine Again

❶ The Wisdom Commentary Vol. 1 (Book/B-136/256pg/52 Topics/$25)

❷ Battle Techniques For War-Weary Saints (Book/B-07/32pg/$5)

❸ Seeds of Wisdom on Overcoming (Book/B-17/32pg/$3)

❹ The Memory Bible on Healing (Book/B-196/32pg/$5)

❺ How To Turn Your Mistakes Into Miracles (Book/B-56/32pg/$5)

❻ 7 Keys To Turning Your Life Around (DVD/MMPL-03D/$10)

❼ The Sun Will Shine Again (Music CD/MMML-01/$10)

Each Wisdom Product may be purchased separately if so desired.

The Wisdom Center
The Turnaround Collection
Only $40 $63 Value
PAK-15
Wisdom Is The Principal Thing

Add 20% For S/H

Financial $ecrets.

THE 31 DAY MENTORSHIP PROGRAM
31 REASONS
PEOPLE DO NOT RECEIVE THEIR
FINANCIAL HARVEST
MIKE MURDOCK

VI-17

VIDEO
7 KEYS to 1000 TIMES MORE
The Lord God Of Your Fathers
Make You A Thousand Times
So Many More As You Are,
And Bless You, As He Hath
Promised You!
Deuteronomy 1:11
MIKE MURDOCK

VI-16

The Wisdom Center
**Buy One...
Receive The
Second One
FREE!**
Wisdom Is The Principal Thing

Your Financial World Will Change Forever.

Video 2-Pak!

▸ 8 Scriptural Reasons You Should Pursue Financial Prosperity

▸ The Secret Prayer Key You Need When Making A Financial Request To God

▸ The Weapon Of Expectation And The 5 Miracles It Unlocks

▸ How To Discern Those Who Qualify To Receive Your Financial Assistance

▸ How To Predict The Miracle Moment God Will Schedule Your Financial Breakthrough

▸ Habits Of Uncommon Achievers

▸ The Greatest Success Law I Ever Discovered

▸ How To Discern Your Place Of Assignment, The Only Place Financial Provision Is Guaranteed

▸ 3 Secret Keys In Solving Problems For Others

The Wisdom Center
Video 2-Pak!
Only **$30** $60 Value
VIPAK-01
Wisdom Is The Principal Thing

Add 20% For S/H

THE WISDOM CENTER
THE WISDOM CENTER   **1-817-759-BOOK**
4051 Denton Highway • Fort Worth, TX 76117   **1-817-759-0300**

You Will Love Our Website...!
WISDOMONLINE.COM

K

THE
WISDOM BIBLE

Partnership Edition

Over 120 Wisdom Study Guides Included Such As:

- ▶ 10 Qualities Of Uncommon Achievers
- ▶ 18 Facts You Should Know About The Anointing
- ▶ 21 Facts To Help You Identify Those Assigned To You
- ▶ 31 Facts You Should Know About Your Assignment
- ▶ 8 Keys That Unlock Victory In Every Attack
- ▶ 22 Defense Techniques To Remember During Seasons Of Personal Attack
- ▶ 20 Wisdom Keys And Techniques To Remember During An Uncommon Battle
- ▶ 11 Benefits You Can Expect From God
- ▶ 31 Facts You Should Know About Favor
- ▶ The Covenant Of 58 Blessings
- ▶ 7 Keys To Receiving Your Miracle
- ▶ 16 Facts You Should Remember About Contentious People
- ▶ 5 Facts Solomon Taught About Contracts
- ▶ 7 Facts You Should Know About Conflict
- ▶ 6 Steps That Can Unlock Your Self-Confidence
- ▶ And Much More!

Your Partnership makes such a difference in The Wisdom Center Outreach Ministries. I wanted to place a Gift in your hand that could last a lifetime for you and your family...**The Wisdom Study Bible.**

40 Years of Personal Notes...this Partnership Edition Bible contains 160 pages of my Personal Study Notes...that could forever change your Bible Study of The Word of God. This **Partnership Edition...**is my personal **Gift of Appreciation** when you sow your Sponsorship Seed of $1,000 to help us complete The Prayer Center and TV Studio Complex. An Uncommon Seed Always Creates An Uncommon Harvest!

Mike

Thank you from my heart for your Seed of Obedience (Luke 6:38).

This Gift Of Appreciation Will Change Your Bible Study For The Rest Of Your Life.

The Wisdom Bible

THE WISDOM CENTER
4051 Denton Highway • Fort Worth, TX 76117

1-817-759-BOOK
1-817-759-0300

You Will Love Our Website...!
WISDOMONLINE.COM

M

Spirit Music.

The Mike Murdock Music Library

LOVE SONGS TO THE HOLY SPIRIT

Written In The Secret Place

TS-59

LOVE SONGS TO THE HOLY SPIRIT
DR. MIKE MURDOCK

THE **HOLY SPIRIT** HANDBOOK

What You Need To Know About Your Daily Companion, The Holy Spirit

The Wisdom Center
Free Book ENCLOSED!
B-100 ($15 Value)
Wisdom Is The Principal Thing

Songs...

1. A Holy Place
2. Anything You Want
3. Everything Comes From You
4. Fill This Place With Your Presence
5. First Thing Every Morning
6. Holy Spirit, I Want To Hear You
7. Holy Spirit, Move Again
8. Holy Spirit, You Are Enough
9. I Don't Know What I Would Do Without You
10. I Let Go (Of Anything That Stops Me)
11. I'll Just Fall On You
12. I Love You, Holy Spirit
13. I'm Building My Life Around You
14. I'm Giving Myself To You
15. I'm In Love! I'm In Love!
16. I Need Water (Holy Spirit, You're My Well)
17. In The Secret Place
18. In Your Presence, I'm Always Changed
19. In Your Presence (Miracles Are Born)
20. I've Got To Live In Your Presence
21. I Want To Hear Your Voice
22. I Will Do Things Your Way
23. Just One Day At A Time
24. Meet Me In The Secret Place
25. More Than Ever Before
26. Nobody Else Does What You Do
27. No No Walls!
28. Nothing Else Matters Anymore (Since I've Been In The Presence Of You Lord)
29. Nowhere Else
30. Once Again You've Answered
31. Only A Fool Would Try (To Live Without You)
32. Take Me Now
33. Teach Me How To Please You
34. There's No Place I'd Rather Be
35. Thy Word Is All That Matters
36. When I Get In Your Presence
37. You're The Best Thing (That's Ever Happened To Me)
38. You Are Wonderful
39. You've Done It Once
40. You Keep Changing Me
41. You Satisfy

The Wisdom Center
6 Tapes / Only $30*
PAK007
Wisdom Is The Principal Thing

Add 20% For S/H